VICTOR SAAD
AND LEAPERS FROM AROUND THE WORLD

FOREWORD BY ALEX BOGUSKY

THE
LEAPYEAR
PROJECT

-Brian

Keep taking
Big Leaps to
attempt great
things!

Nate B

DESIGN
Grip
1128 North Ashland Avenue
Chicago Illinois 60622
USA
www.gripdesign.com

PRINTING
Graphic Arts Studio
28W111 Commercial Avenue
Barrington Illinois 60010
USA
www.gasink.net

PAPER
This book was printed on Utopia Two Matte 100lb Text and Utopia Two Dull 120lb Cover, manufactured by Appleton Coated.

EDITING
Ben Skoda & Tyler Savage
WRITTEN WITH
Michelle Lincoln & Tyler Savage
COPYEDITING
Johnny Michael & Ben Skoda

COVER PHOTO
Daniel Kelleghan

First Printing, 2013
ISBN 978-0-9892230-2-7

The Leap Year Project
www.leapyearproject.org

For My Mom.

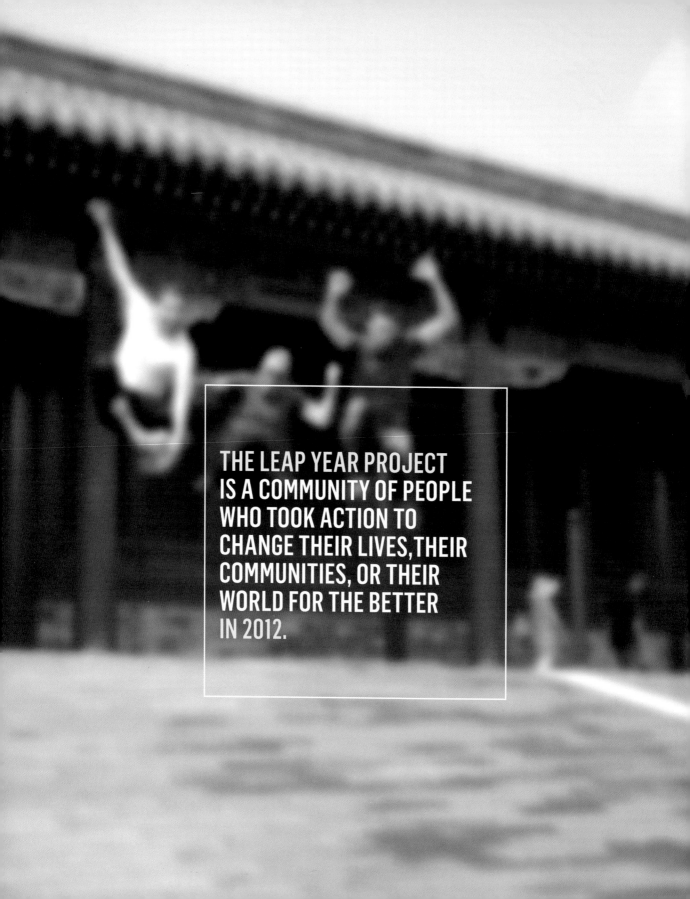

THE LEAP YEAR PROJECT
IS A COMMUNITY OF PEOPLE
WHO TOOK ACTION TO
CHANGE THEIR LIVES, THEIR
COMMUNITIES, OR THEIR
WORLD FOR THE BETTER
IN 2012.

JAN
12

FEB
24

MAR
36

APR
48

MAY
60

JUN
72

JUL
94

AUG
106

SEP
118

OCT
130

NOV
144

DEC
158

Thanks to our generous sponsors. This wouldn't be possible without you.

Maddock Douglas
Agency of Innovation®

Joe & Amanda
Cassidy

There are two kinds of days that make up our lives. Those days of big decisions and change. And the days in between. This book is a story about both of those sorts of days, and how to make the most of each.

If you desire to have an average life, you should focus just on the big decisions. Then in between those big decision days, keep your nose clean and do your 9 to 5. That's right. Focus on those big decision moments and the best you can hope for is a mediocre existence. Seems sort of backwards, but there you have it.

So how about an above average life? Well, for an above average life, don't sweat the big decisions. Just go with the flow. But, and this is a big but, show up for each day in between like it's the only day you'll ever have. In the end you will end up miles ahead of the "big decision" folks.

Why? Probably, it's just math. Because no matter how good you are at making big decisions you'll only have a handful or so your whole life to make. Maybe 5 to 10 big decision days where you get to really shine. Now those in-between days are going to be a whole lot more numerous. Statistically, figure you'll get 30,000 of those in-between days. Even if you take off weekends, holidays and lots of personal days, you can easily crush 15,000 days. So clearly, the odds are in the favor of the people who show up big every day.

Now, what if you want something even better than an above average life? What if you want to live an extraordinary life? Well, then you'll need to focus on both kinds of days. Those big decision days and each and every "in-between" day.

What you'll see in the pages of this book is the story of a young man doing just that. Victor has made some courageous big decisions, but even more impressive than that is how he showed up each day. In fact, after his time with us, I referred to him as "The Greatest Intern, ever."

But his real contribution goes way beyond the work he did with companies like ours and just might have more to do with you. Yeah, you. Because along the way, Victor has uncovered an approach to higher education that might be **your first step into an extraordinary life.**

ALEX BOGUSKY

07

LEARNING TO RISK

This adventure all started with a single, deep-seated desire — to make a difference.

After graduating from college, I spent the next several years working with middle school and high school students in the western suburbs of Chicago. During that time I began learning about social enterprise; a way for businesses to use their products and profits to do good.

I was hooked.

It seemed that going back to school for an MBA was the most obvious option. Having grown up in a Middle Eastern family where the expectation was to become a doctor, lawyer, or engineer, I thought further education might make up for not having pursued one of those more traditional routes.

But the cost of a degree was way more than I could afford, and I wondered if business school was actually the most effective way for me to learn.

There had to be another way.

I began dreaming about a self-made education; books I would read, people I could work with, conferences I should attend.

I started calling my idea The Leap Year Project and shared it with hundreds of people, asking each one for feedback and advice. Most thought I was crazy — ambitious, but crazy. In nearly every interview, I closed with one final question: "What would you do if you could take a risk to change your life, your community, or your world for the better?"

The responses were honest and meaningful. They ranged from personal projects, to business ventures, to community-centered endeavors. But most people claimed that money, age, or lack of time posed too many hurdles.

Through those conversations, I realized that creating any sort of change would not be easy. This idea of a self-made education was possible, but I would have to be all in.

Since fully investing in the project would mean leaving my job, I recognized the need to create some sort of structure. The format I chose was twelve experiences in twelve months.

I picked my 'classrooms' for the year by identifying people or organizations that I felt had something to teach me in the areas of design, business, and social change.

As I prepared to take this leap, a friend informed me that the following year was actually a Leap Year. It was too perfect.

Things were coming together.

RISKING TO LEARN

THE LEAPERS

At the same time, I began wondering what would happen if other people also used this year to attempt the leaps they were dreaming about. So a few friends and I launched a Leap Year Project website to invite others to join us.

As people from all over the world stumbled across the project, accepted the invitation, and shared their stories, a community of 'Leapers' began to develop. While each individual's leap was unique, we shared the common bond of taking a risk to learn and attempt something great.

THE TEAM

In addition to the amazing Leapers, an invested community of supporters, friends, and volunteers began to form. A group of nearly 100 people financially supported the project, while others offered lodging, meals, standby flights, or other resources. A few hard-working people even joined a team of friends who worked behind the scenes; creating the designs, managing social media, and compiling this book.

Without these wonderful and generous people, none of this would have been possible.

THE BOOK

As you read on, you'll discover that The Leap Year Project has been quite the adventure. Each chapter contains a piece of my story, a brief summary of my educational experience for that month, followed by the stories of Leapers from around the world. We couldn't include every word from every Leaper, but you can read their entire story online at www.leapyearproject.org.

Our hope is that this book will be a companion on your journey; a tool for the moments when you are stuck, facing a problem, dreaming about the future, or simply on the brink of something great. May it push you to see the need for change and join with others to do great things, together.

HAPPY LEAPING!
Victor

SUPERHEROES
AND
DISHWASHERS

DOEJO
CHICAGO, IL

I'M A NERD. YOU NEED TO KNOW THAT ABOUT ME.

I LOVE SUPERHEROES, I HAVE AN AMAZING RANGE OF PERSONALIZED SOUND EFFECTS, AND I MAY OR MAY NOT HAVE A CONCRETE BUSINESS PLAN FOR LAUNCHING MY OWN CAPE COMPANY.

But my fascination with superheroes goes far beyond the costume. I love the idea of changing the world, and there are times when I am certain of my superpowers; ready to leap over tall buildings and bend large metal objects.

I'd be lying if I didn't admit The Leap Year Project was born out of this boyish aspiration to change the world and my unwavering belief that together, we could do extraordinary things. I had no idea what to expect when I began creating my own education, but I quickly envisioned the spectacular — empowering people to realize their own superpowers and do the impossible.

LITTLE DID I KNOW, IN THE VERY FIRST MONTH, THOSE DREAMS AND IDEAS WOULD UNDERGO A DRASTIC RESTRUCTURING.

UNEXPECTED BEGINNINGS

Soon after I started looking for the twelve different companies or experiences that would be my classrooms for the year, a mentor and close friend introduced me to an entrepreneur named Phil Tadros.

Phil had started several successful coffee shops and was about to launch an incredible new line of coffee. Shadowing him would give me firsthand experience in the entrepreneurial world. It seemed like the perfect start for my self-made MBA.

Exchanging emails, I could tell he was open but also somewhat apprehensive. He repeatedly warned me he was 'unconventional.' Trying to put him at ease, I explained I'd do my best to not get in the way.

January 7th, my first day, came quickly and neither of us knew what to expect. Arriving early at the address Phil had given me, I walked through a narrow hallway, climbed an unfinished flight of stairs, and opened the door into a gorgeous office space full of people working fervently on beautiful computers.

"Where am I?" I thought to myself. "Does this guy have an entire team of people that help him with his coffee shops? That IS unconventional."

I sat, waited, and wondered.

Phil walked in working on his phone, greeted me, and I awkwardly followed him to his desk.

We didn't know anything about each other and we didn't know where to start. He was busy. I felt like I was intruding.

"How about a quick tour?" he asked, reaching for any opportunity to move things forward.

"That would be great!"

The office space was still under construction. Pointing to a specific room he explained, "Soon, this will be Doejo's full video editing suite."

"Cool." I said. "What's Doejo?"

"What?! Doejo is my main gig. It's my digital agency — designers, programmers, videographers, business consultants. You didn't know about Doejo? The coffee thing is just one of my side projects."

I was floored. I thought Phil was simply 'the coffee guy.' But I had stumbled into exactly the kind of place I had hoped to learn from this year, and I didn't even know it existed!

HOW CAN I HELP?

Walking into Doejo was eye opening. My first days were spent learning names, positions, and projects. Everyone was focused on fueling new, good ideas — creating tools and products for other people. They were hard at work, and no one really knew what to do with me or my project.

In the meantime, Phil was almost impossible to keep up with. He told me to follow him out the door whenever he left for meetings; I quickly found out just how uncomfortable that could be. Several times, unable to muster the courage, I remained stuck to my chair as I watched him leave the room.

Unanswered questions crowded my mind.

What should I focus on each day? Who was my direct report? What did success look like?

Phil's answer every time was, "You'll figure it out."

I still had visions of spectacular change and learning experiences that I hoped would take place, but quickly realized this year was going to be much more about being helpful than being spectacular.

JAN 05

@victorsaad: The #lyproject tag is going nuts. 100s of tweets! Whatever happens, hopefully people are thinking thru their own risks for good in 2012!

I had to come to grips with the uncertainty and just get started. I had to learn how to glean lessons from any and every experience, rather than relying on a teacher with a plan. Nothing was beneath me — everything was an opportunity to learn.

"How can I help?" became my motto, my inspiration, my starting point.

Since the office was under construction, I noticed a lot of things were missing or needed a place. This was my first mission — trash cans, plates, cleaning supplies, etc. Within the first week, I understood the office flow and got used to the chaos.

By week two, Phil and I discovered a mutual interest in cause-based creative work and started discussing a small design team staffed by interns that could handle more non-profit and community projects. The idea for the Doejo Foundation was born.

As he continued to push me to "figure it out," I spent a lot of time prototyping; meeting with lawyers, writing business plans, and working with designers. But even with this fun and newfound direction, there was nothing more beneficial than finding small ways to help.

If a light bulb was out, I would replace it. If a printer was broken, I'd try to fix it (and often fail). If they needed someone to answer phones or greet clients as they walked through the doors, I was there.

On any given day, I could be a custodian, repairman, or receptionist.

IT STARTS WITH ME

Every month, I sought opportunities wherever help was needed; late night conversations, buying coffee, design changes, website layout, renovation, filmwork, community building, listening to rants and raves, smiling.

The experience and skills I gained at Doejo were incredibly valuable, but I was learning it was the simple acts that became defining, not exactly superpowers. My hopes to change the world were only as important as my willingness to use my own two hands. I learned the simplest place to start was with me.

Change happens slowly and is rarely glamorous. Innovative ideas and great systems are necessary — but they are not the starting point. I'm the starting point — you're the starting point.

Now... back to my plans for the cape company!

FIGURE IT OUT.

JAN 13

The greatest journeys come with the willingness to take the first step...

The greatest destinations come with the courage to continue until the last.

JAN 18

About to speak at a career night. I find that funny. "Hi kids, I quit my job to give away an idea and create my own MBA. Any questions?"

One down ... eleven to go!

AURORA
IL
USA

MAKE MYSELF VULNERABLE. STEP ONE: NO MAKEUP MONTH

When I was chosen out of an international competition to spend 100 days living with indigenous tribes in the oldest rainforest on the planet and raise awareness about deforestation, I threw caution, a Capitol Hill job, stability and common sense to the wind. I took the leap! At the start of 2012, I packed my bags for Borneo, Indonesia and began a season of adventure, service, and learning.

Making this decision didn't come without anxiety and plenty of sleepless nights. My last day at my job on Capitol Hill was nothing short of terrifying. But once I arrived in Borneo and saw my first orphaned orangutan, witnessed the destruction we are causing this planet with my own eyes, lived among the Dayaks and learned their way of life, I was filled with a sense of calm.

I haven't shown up to school or work without makeup in years. I just don't do it. I think it's a lack of self-confidence, but that's something I'm working on. I guess I don't feel beautiful without makeup, and that's why I'm participating in No Makeup Month. In preparation, I took a photo of myself sans-makeup, posted it to Facebook, and a lot of people posted what a great idea they thought it was, and some even took up the initiative themselves. When I saw that others were taking up the challenge and encouraging others to do it, that was the most rewarding moment for me. I adopted a sort of "así es la vida" (such is life) attitude about it all, and just went with it. In the end, it was all worth it.

LEAVE THE HALLS OF CONGRESS FOR THE JUNGLES OF BORNEO TO HELP STOP DEFORESTATION

LIZA HEAVENER
WASHINGTON, DC * USA

TO MAKE MORE ART & SPUR CREATIVE ACTION IN OTHERS

KATIE HERMAN
CHICAGO, IL * USA

I came to the realization that I'd much rather live with disappointing outcomes rather than regret or uncertainty. If you try something and it's not what you expect, you may be disappointed, but you can move on. If you only think about doing something, the grey area is always going to be there, looming, shadowing, making you question.

And after you say yes a few times, even to those things that are so incredibly scary, you'll start to notice that a) it gets easier to jump, and b) more often than not, the result will be even more than you had hoped for.

A year later, it's been the best move. I'm learning that I live the most charmed life ever. Even with whatever bumps may arise, life is good. It's amazing what transpires when you say yes.

LEAVE BEHIND WHAT'S BEEN MY FULL TIME WORK TO SEE IF I COULD COACH PEOPLE TO LIVE A MORE MEANINGFUL LIFE OF SAYING YES!

SAYA HILLMAN
CHICAGO, IL * USA

This is the year I believed I could write 52 pieces of music in 52 weeks.

Everyone has fantasies, right? I mean, in my wildest dreams, one of my musical heroes would say, "You're just the guy I've been looking for," and offer me a gig. What actually happened was that people were moved. They connected on an emotional level; and that's all any writer of any stripe can ever hope to have. That connection.

CHICAGO
IL
USA

A YEAR IN MUSIC.
A SONG A WEEK,
WRITTEN,
PRODUCED &
RECORDED BY ME

THE
CHALLENGE
OF HOPE

PLYWOOD PEOPLE
ATLANTA, GA

+

CAIRO, EGYPT

I'VE ALWAYS BEEN HOPEFUL.

Growing up, my life was far from perfect. My own broken family, and seeing others struggling with significant pain, confirmed early on that happy endings weren't exactly the norm.

Thankfully, there were great people around me — teachers, pastors, friends — who inspired me to look for hope even in seemingly hopeless situations. It was their influence that helped me find my own path to make an impact.

From the time I was very young, I was expected to one day be Dr. Victor Saad. I still remember preparing to tell my family it wasn't for me. Fearing it would be just one more disappointment, I hesitantly explained to my (then divorced) parents my desire to work with students experiencing the same struggles I had. It was a tough conversation, but to my surprise, they gave me their blessing.

It turned out to be the right decision. When I left for college, my parents began to spend time with the same hopeful people who invested in my life. Not long after, I received an unexpected phone call from my dad.

"Victor!" he said in his quiet, Arabic accent, "She said yes!"

They were remarried after six years apart and it remains one of the most incredible things that has ever happened in our family.

The choice to follow my own path wasn't what brought my parents back together. But the common thread, in my leap and in theirs, was the inspiration we drew from the people around us who helped us see past great obstacles.

IN LIFE, OBSTACLES ARE EVERYWHERE, THE CHALLENGE IS TO REMAIN HOPEFUL.

AN UNEXPECTED INVITATION

Hi Victor.

I hope you're doing well. As I've been thinking about a new retreat I'm creating with Plywood People, and the people who I think it could really benefit, you came to mind.

I wanted to personally invite you to attend. I think it could be really helpful to what you're doing this year.

Let me know what you think,
Jeff

I'd met Jeff Shinabarger the previous year and he'd quickly become someone I wanted to learn from, but wasn't sure how — his email was both surprising and exciting.

I knew instantly that I wanted to go to the retreat, but as February grew closer, I was already struggling to maintain the balance between my educational experiences and the growing administrative side of The Leap Year Project.

I knew making the trip would be worthwhile, so I headed south with anticipation.

Set on a gorgeous, 700-acre farm just outside of Atlanta, the retreat was an incredible four days with fifteen bright, passionate, creative, and hopeful individuals.

We dove into sessions covering business plan development, branding/marketing, societal rhythms, fundraising practices, idea implementation, and my personal favorite — whimsy.

Every session was inspiring. Every conversation left me encouraged.

The time with Jeff and the crew set me ablaze, like standing in the middle of a dark room with a thousand sparklers simultaneously erupting. Laying awake each night, I thought about ways I could grow the project and use it to instill hope in others.

During one conversation, I shared my concerns, as an Egyptian American, surrounding the political and social unrest accompanying the Arab Spring in Egypt. Too often, the bad news from the region was overwhelming — it felt as if no one was highlighting the people doing good.

I told my newfound friends about my growing plan to find and share inspiring, positive news from Egypt while spreading The Leap Year Project in that part of the world. Organizing a trip to the Middle East on short notice was a crazy idea, but they encouraged me not to let it go.

Visiting Egypt was a leap I needed to take.

HOPE AND ITS RIVALS

As hopeful as I was, planning and pulling off this trip was a serious challenge and I couldn't do it alone. I wanted to capture a lot of footage, so I knew there was only one person I could call.

A friend from college, Tyler Jackson, and I have taken a number of spontaneous trips together. Whether it was D.C. on a whim or snowboarding in the Rockies, Tyler was always up for it. He also happens to be one of the most talented people I know with a camera.

All it took was one quick call and he was in.

Six days and a whirlwind of planning later, we were on a flight to Cairo.

We could have powered an entire city block with the charge of optimism and excitement flowing between us. I was nervous taking my friend into an unknown environment with $10,000 worth of camera gear on our shoulders, but we were fueled by a deep sense of adventure.

Our hopes took several hits in the first few days. We were threatened in Tahrir square, paid for a certain 'filming license' that was never used, and witnessed the aftermath of fear and hate.

FEB 05

@victorsaad: Just got the most thorough pat down of my life. I feel like I should shower. And...talk to a therapist.

FEB 13

Filled with Hope, we work towards change. Inspired by one another, we dare to create

29

On the third day, we woke up to capture footage as the sun was rising. While we unloaded our camera equipment, two young boys started to talk with us. They left soon after, but came back with two more boys — bigger boys.

We took footage of them leaping, something we did in every location, and didn't think anything of it.

But a few minutes later my cousin Fady came rushing over to ask, "Are you guys ok?" We didn't understand why he was worried.

"My mechanic said two boys were gathering a group of friends to take your camera gear, but he told them you were with me so they didn't go through with it."

I was floored.

Disappointment, frustration, even anger started to well up inside me. I struggled with it for the next few hours. It was one of those times this entire project seemed foolish.

Wrestling with disappointment and defeat, I realized those boys not only nearly stole our gear, they nearly stole our hope.

THOSE BOYS NOT ONLY NEARLY STOLE OUR GEAR, THEY NEARLY STOLE OUR HOPE.

VISIT INSPIRATION OFTEN

While in Cairo, my amazing cousin Fady was our driver, bodyguard, and cultural guide. He was also an honest voice with respect to the entire project.

Fady was skeptical we'd find many hopeful stories amidst the political and social unrest. With a 60% unemployment rate and a shaky Egyptian military in Cairo, hope seemed outmatched.

Enter Wellspring Egypt.

A non-profit using experiential learning and athletics to teach students strong values, life skills, and character building. We learned the entire Wellspring staff had left lucrative careers to work with students in schools and universities around Cairo.

Fady was fascinated by this group and sat in on every story we filmed, each more inspiring than the one before.

I will never forget what he said over lunch afterward. "Those stories! I had no idea people like that existed. Now I understand why you're here." Seeing his enthusiasm and understanding reminded me of the hope that had inspired our trip.

With the right perspective, the biggest obstacles or challenges can become opportunities for discovering hope. Hope has a beginning, it has a source, and for each of us that source is different. It could be a mentor, your faith, stories like Wellspring Egypt, an experience, or even the story of a broken relationship being mended.

There is a fine line between inspiration and disappointment. You might dance back and forth over that line on a daily basis, but the deciding factor on where you land is likely determined by hope.

Where does your hope, your inspiration, come from?

Know the source and visit it often.

Hope
14

Challenge
10

FEB 29

Sweet. #lyproject meetup in Paris just started. 10 months... what will they attempt and what stories will they share? #doinggood #together

31

While spending a semester in Bangkok, Thailand, I was introduced to the issue of commercial sex trafficking. The point of no return for me was when some friends and I decided to go to a karaoke bar and upon arrival discovered it was a brothel, not karaoke. It broke me to know that many of these young girls were there by force. This is when I decided to take my leap.

I set up an organization to provide job opportunities for at-risk women and refugees of the commercial sex trade through creating high-quality handmade products.

It's been challenging, but I've reazlied that it's not about fixing the whole issue, but about taking each step in front of you. Eventually all of those steps combined will get you to a place where you have influence in the arena that you are passionate about.

$\longrightarrow$

GROVE CITY
PA
USA

START AN ORGANIZATION TO BRING ECONOMIC OPPORTUNITIES TO VICTIMS OF THE GLOBAL COMMERCIAL SEX TRAFFICKING INDUSTRY

HELP CHILDREN AROUND THE WORLD BY GIVING THEM A NEW PAIR OF SHOES

**GIOVANNA MEZA
CHICAGO, IL ∗ USA**

We've started in Colombia's northern coastal region and reached out to the neediest of children lacking one basic necessity: shoes.

These shoes give children a sense that they belong to a larger world that cares. For us, the challenge was one that seemed hopeless. Getting shoes to South America seemed impossible, not only because it was far, but because if sent, the shoes could have been stolen and sold. With little hope in our hearts we thought it'd never happen. The title for this leap, Torn Little Shoe, was inspired by the Spanish nursery rhyme "Zapatico Roto." It was while thinking and singing the nursery rhyme that we realized how fast time flies, how fast children grow and how important it was to pursue this project. Our brainstorming session delivered a simple answer: Stuff suitcases with as many shoes as we could. Our compensation? A smiling child.

←

→

This year, my family and friends asked me what I was doing for my Golden Birthday, and like many budding social entrepreneurs before me, I decided to forgo gifts and, instead, raise money for a cause that has pulled at me for as long as I can remember. I am starting a higher education scholarship fund through an organization changing the playing field for girls in the developing world, Edge of Seven. What started as a 25-day campaign to raise $2,500 by my 25th birthday is now in a process of transformation. All of this is laying a foundation in my mind about how I can continue to do this work as I pursue a medical career, and I plan to continue it in the future.

USE MY GOLDEN BIRTHDAY TO RAISE $2,500 IN SCHOLARSHIPS FOR GIRLS IN THE DEVELOPING WORLD

**VICKI LAWN
PHILADELPHIA, PA ∗ USA**

PROVIDE AN INTEGRATED SUMMER CAMP FOR ARAB & JEWISH YOUTH IN JERUSALEM

→

∧

A few weeks before our first summer camp was scheduled to begin, we received a devastating email which stated, in broken English, that we couldn't hold camp because the school facilities were going to be under construction. After a few moments of breathless panic, we simply decided we had come too far to give up. We soon reached out to our other contacts in Jerusalem to begin the process of finding a new space.

We visited a number of different community centers in the area and eventually settled on one that offered us a room. We took what we could get!

I guess this project is sort of like a relationship in that way — every day you decide to recommit.

CHICAGO
IL
USA

I lost my hope in Ethiopia. I felt like I was everybody's ATM. The locals all thought I was rich, but I only had a limited budget donated from friends and family, so every penny counted. I got extorted multiple times, was beat over the head with a bottle, my buddy was stabbed in a fight, and we both ended up in a dangerous situation out in the jungle involving a crooked police chief, a shady goods broker, and a crime boss who ran a local village. AND I was chased by a hyena one night! Yes, Ethiopia was tough. And I started to hate people. The one local I trusted, Alazar, was really what brought me out of it. He was a kind ear that listened, and he looked at me as a person and not as an American object. He made the trip worth it. We are friends to this day, and he is still saving money to get his own camera so he can become a photographer in Ethiopia.

CHICAGO
IL
USA

TRAVEL TO ETHIOPIA & KENYA
FOR 6 MONTHS IN 2012 TO HELP 2 NGOS
DEVELOP THEIR FUNDRAISING &
MARKETING INITIATIVES

TOGETHER

———

THREADLESS
CHICAGO, IL

LONE RANGER

I NEVER WANTED TO BE A LONE RANGER, LAUNCHING SOME IDEALISTIC, WORLD-CHANGING PIPEDREAM.

THE MOTIVATION BEHIND THE LEAP YEAR PROJECT WAS ACTUALLY TO CREATE A SPACE FOR ORDINARY, HOPEFUL PEOPLE LIKE ME TO EXPLORE WAYS THEY COULD MAKE THE WORLD BETTER.

Finding and connecting those people, however, was a much more difficult and lonely process than I ever imagined. Explaining the idea was challenging, and it took me far outside my comfort zone.

As I began asking friends and family to plan their own leaps for 2012, I knew if I couldn't explain the idea well enough to get them to join, then I was in trouble.

Over the first few months, I spoke with anyone who would listen to the idea. At one point I was meeting with forty to fifty people a week. Initially progress was slow, but eventually the pieces started to come together, and we began to see Leapers connecting with each other and forming a community.

One of two things happens when you step out of your comfort zone. Either the help you need seemingly appears out of nowhere, or you're forced to become creative and persistent in making connections with the right people.

March, for me, was an example of both.

39

THE LONG SHOTS

Before the project began, we sent personalized videos to thirty influential leaders, actors, musicians, and politicians — including the President.

We spent hours shooting and editing the footage, and delivered the videos every way we knew how: emails, packages, tweets, and notes to friends, co-workers, and agents.

We're still waiting to hear back from most of them...

One of our targets was a Chicago-based company that had achieved hero status in my mind: Threadless.

Pioneers of crowdsourcing as a business model, Threadless is a community-driven design and apparel company known for building community, fostering creativity, and supporting worthy causes with their brand.

I knew working with Threadless was a bit of a long shot, but a few days after we shot the videos, I was at a conference where Threadless' CEO, Tom Ryan, was being interviewed.

As he was wrapping up, I instinctively began moving towards what I thought was his most likely exit. Surprisingly, I chose correctly and after a brief conversation, Tom agreed to meet with me at Threadless.

During our meeting, he was kind enough to discuss my project in more detail and invited me to send him more information describing how we might partner.

I had only forty-eight hours before catching a flight home for the holidays, but I gathered some materials and started cutting and pasting together a video proposal. It was one of those late night projects that left shreds of paper and empty coffee cups strewn across my apartment, and amazingly it led to a meeting with one of the founders of Threadless, Jake Nickell.

As we discussed different ideas, Jake became especially interested in my self-made MBA and told me I should spend some time at Threadless.

It was a dream opportunity for me.

I went home and cleared every appointment and travel date for the month of March.

THE THREADLESS COMMUNITY

A company adopts the culture of the people who lead it. This was evident at Threadless.

It didn't take long to see that Jake and Tom's love for their team and invested leadership had created a culture where people work well together.

Every surface of the office space is covered with monsters, murals, witty phrases, and quirky drawings. And whether it was throwing parties, hosting movie nights, grilling at lunch, or accidentally making the women's bathroom smell like gasoline for two days, the staff's imagination and zest for life wasn't stifled by their work — it fueled their work.

In addition to the open and fun environment, Threadless rallies around their vibrant community of artists and supporters. With over 2.5 million members submitting artwork and/or voting for their favorite designs, they are widespread, creative, and powerful.

Jake would often tell me, "This is far less about t-shirts, and far more about helping artists share their work."

This investment in people has allowed the Threadless community to reach millions of members, and is why it continues to grow.

A COMPANY ADOPTS THE CULTURE OF THE PEOPLE WHO LEAD IT.

MAR 02

@victorsaad: Early morning 10 mile bike ride to work. Talked to mom the entire way! So fun to finally share all the stories with her! Best mom ever.

MAR 07

Oh man, being the new guy can be super tricky. #lyproject #learning

41

RELATIONSHIPS ARE THE MOST POWERFUL ENGINES FOR CHANGE.

BUILDING PARTNERSHIPS

Jake and I laid out six projects to tackle in five weeks including research, writing proposals, and managing design challenges.

I realized this was a grand undertaking, and although I was excited to get started, I was again faced with the prospect of being the new guy. In one of the most creative companies in the world, it was hard not to feel intimidated, but I kept reminding myself to learn all I could about building good teams and good community.

One of my tasks was to research and categorize past and current Threadless partnerships, then brainstorm new partnerships for each category. Everyone was busy, so there would be no extensive group whiteboarding sessions. But I needed input from others, and soon learned that people appreciated quick, worthwhile conversations.

Embracing the value of these creative distractions proved to be a helpful and fun way to ease in quickly during each of my experiences throughout the year.

I learned how to take the scraps of several conversations and serve up well-researched solutions to a problem, all while giving credit to the people around me who had actually come up with the ideas.

My focus on Threadless' partnerships allowed me to contribute to the team, and gave them a fresh perspective on one of their company's core values. It even led to an exciting partnership with The Leap Year Project: a design challenge called *Taking Leaps*.

FORMING COMMUNITY

While all of this was happening at Threadless, The Leap Year Project was quickly developing a thriving community.

We assembled a small team to manage social media and develop a website where people could share the stories of their Leaps.

Leapers were connecting and collaborating with each other, and new ideas and partnerships were starting to multiply.

It wasn't just me and a few friends anymore.

The team met nearly every week to brainstorm, design, write newsletters, plan our next steps, share stories, celebrate, and laugh.

On the 29th of February, we hosted Leap Day Meetups. These gatherings took place literally all over the world to share stories and discuss the question, "What Leap will you take?"

From our meetup in downtown Chicago we got wind of a dinner in Paris, a wine night in Germany, and gatherings in Austin, LA, Seattle, even Japan — 39 cities in 8 countries.

It was the first time since I left my job that I actually felt a team was forming, and nothing could have been more empowering.

BETTER TOGETHER

It's no secret that I'm an extrovert. I have always loved being around people, but in March I was reminded that relationships are the most powerful engines for change.

One of the major factors in whatever leap you take is the people you surround yourself with; your family, friends, co-workers, mentor, spouse, or anyone who has an influence on you.

Hope is contagious — we inspire each other with every leap we take, big or small — and as I looked around our team meetings, I realized this entire project was built on friendship. We had little money or reputation, but we did have big ideas, lots of hope, and a good dose of fun.

And that's all we needed.

Together, we were making something great.

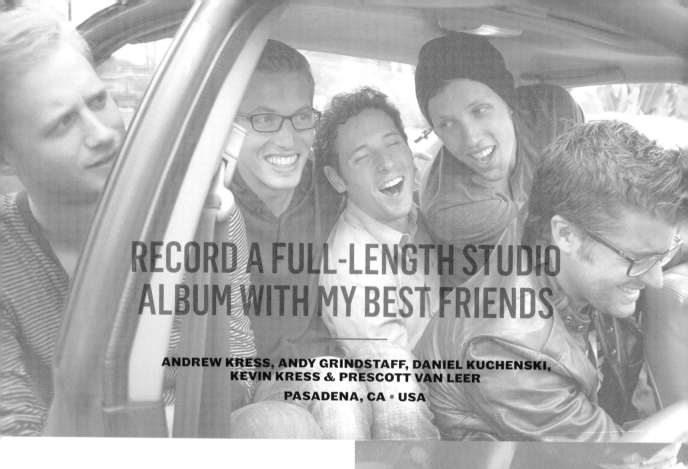

RECORD A FULL-LENGTH STUDIO ALBUM WITH MY BEST FRIENDS

ANDREW KRESS, ANDY GRINDSTAFF, DANIEL KUCHENSKI, KEVIN KRESS & PRESCOTT VAN LEER

PASADENA, CA * USA

Since starting in 2002, our band "Five Mile Town" always had two resolutions: to one day record a full-length album, and to never let our friendships take a backseat to the band. And so began our journey...

Every night we left completely exhausted, but every morning we couldn't wait to get back in the studio. It was one of the best months of our lives. Not just because of our love for the music itself, but because it marks the fulfillment of a decade-long dream. A dream that, as we learned, was accomplished not because of talent or resources, but because of others' help and a tight-knit friendship that was determined to collaborate on something that lasts. When we take a step back and listen to the final product, we can't believe that we actually made it. Our dream took 10 years to realize and a year to complete, but it was worth every second.

USE MY LOVE OF SANDWICHES TO BRING PEOPLE TOGETHER & SHARE AWESOME CONVERSATIONS AROUND THE DINNER TABLE

THE BETTER TOGETHER TOUR

KLAYTON KORVER
ALEXANDRA NELSON
TODD PINCKNEY
KELLY CAMPBELL
CHICAGO, IL * USA

CHICAGO
IL
USA

This idea started with four friends who wanted to find fierce, soft voices of people pursuing hopeful, restorative work in dark places.

We did the next logical thing — bought an RV to travel the country for six weeks in order to find and tell the stories of people who see beauty in their broken communities.

We have had the honor of interviewing electricians and filmmakers, writers and artists, builders and pastors, college students with huge, inspired ideas, musicians, families, and all sorts of people using their God-given gifts to serve and be a part of the movement of hope and restoration sweeping our nation.

These stories of transformation, hope, and redemption surround us. But the thing is, you may never know about them, because oftentimes the people living them are too busy serving others to seek glory for themselves. There is something about these people and their stories; they're the men and women we wish we were more like, the ones living stories and lives bigger than themselves.

And that was our mission — to find these stories.

CREATE OUR
OWN BUSINESS
TOGETHER &
LIVE HALFWAY
ACROSS THE
WORLD

LAURA & XAVIER PAVIA
VALENCIA * SPAIN

Here's how it happened:

MARGARET: Ew. Are we going to have to start online dating?

BECCA: Gross. I would never go on an online date unless you came with.

MARGARET: Seriously. Me neither.

So there you have it, a dream was born.

Up until our crowdfunding campaign the two of us were the only ones who had invested anything into this, but suddenly nearly 60 of our friends and family members were invested as well. There was no turning back after that.

We challenge each other, focus each other, and propel each other forward. We have fun together and spark creativity in one another as we work. Without that, neither of us can imagine maintaining the enthusiasm required to drive the project forward month after month.

∨

FIND MY TRIBE

LEAH MARSHALL
CHICAGO, IL * USA

∧

START A START-UP

MARGARET RODE & BECCA FEROE
CHICAGO, IL * USA

To connect with others, I signed up to restore hiking trails in the Virgin Islands National Park, registered for West Coast Swing dance lessons, joined a non-profit advisory board, and started mentoring an extraordinary 10-year-old.

While restoring hiking trails, I found the nature of the work united us in a really unique and unexpected way. Personality quirks became endearing. Everyone brought their own strengths and skills to the table.

I think what made the experience so rich was that we connected because of our differences. This realization helped me understand what being part of a tribe is all about: it's getting to be an individual yet feeling deeply connected to others, it's feeling safe in the midst of risk-taking and the unexpected, and it's pushing yourself to be better because of the people you're with.

GOOD THINGS
TAKE TIME

LA CHOZA DEL
MUNDO
COSTA RICA

LET ME EXPLAIN

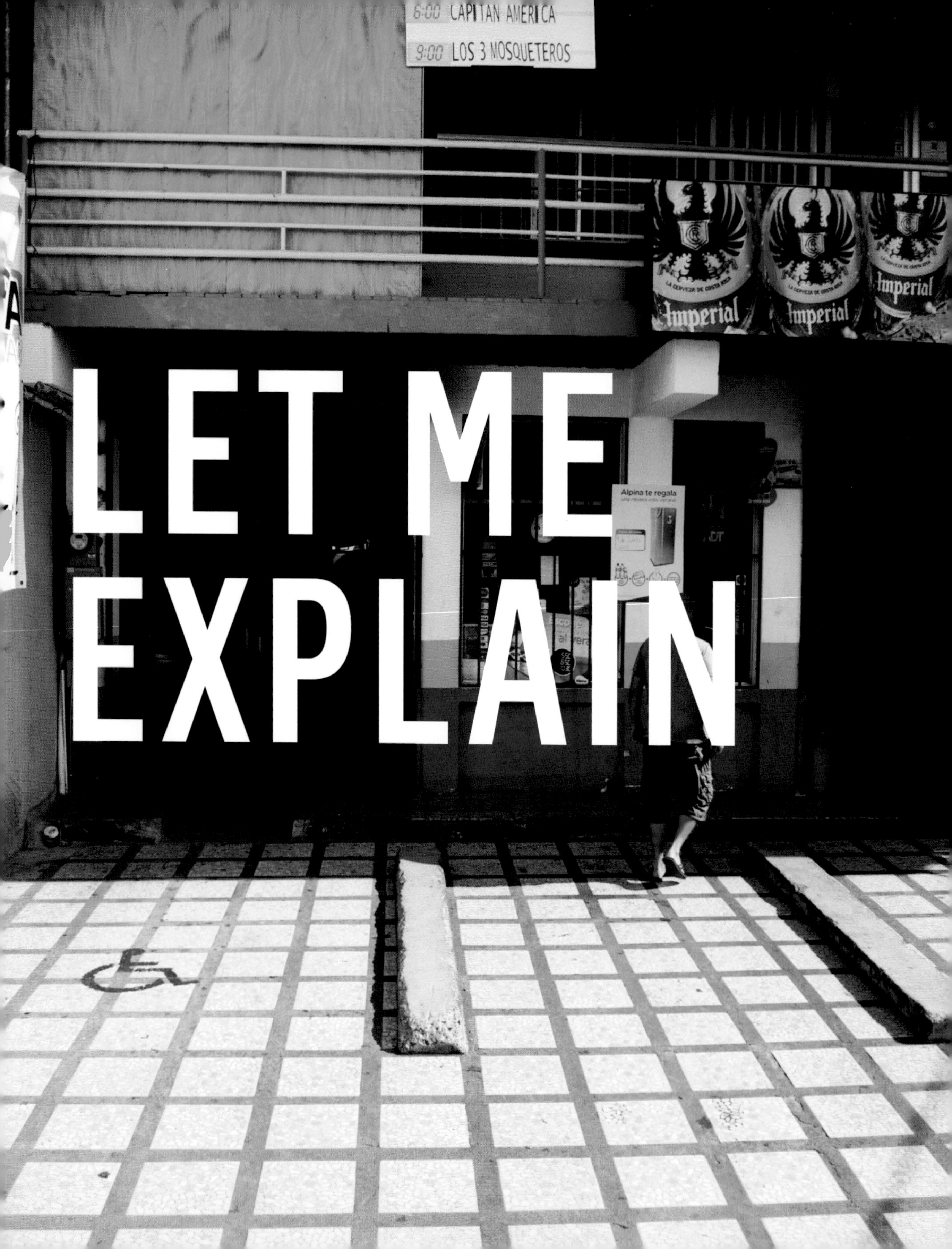

SAYING NO IS HARD. SAYING NO TO THIS SEEMED BORDERLINE CRAZY.

———————

LET ME EXPLAIN.

As my time at Threadless came to an end, we began discussing the possibility of staying on staff with the Community Partnerships Team and phasing out the education side of The Leap Year Project early.

The position was a perfect fit, the work was meaningful, and I really respected the team.

It was hard to imagine passing up a well-paying job at a great company in my favorite city, but as I spoke with a few of my closest friends, we all shared a gut feeling that it was better not to stop early, that I needed to continue the project.

I wasn't sure which I would regret more, staying or going, but eventually I decided that I must fulfill my commitment to giving The Leap Year Project my absolute best shot, and that meant saying no.

IT WAS TIME FOR APRIL.

SOCIAL CHANGE AND FARMING?

Although it was easier to find experiences exploring design, business, and social change that followed the five-day workweek, nine-to-five schedule, I also wanted to make sure those weren't my only experiences throughout the year.

When a friend of mine, Mariah Savage, told me about her upcoming internship as a host and activity manager at La Choza del Mundo, a unique, organic farm in Costa Rica, I was intrigued.

The farm was started by four friends who met while working for space industry giants like NASA and Virgin Galactic. After discovering a mutual interest in individual and community development, they purchased the farm to create a place of learning and growth, where people could collaborate, build relationships, and work on implementing great ideas.

For Mariah, it fit her interests in international development, organic lifestyle, and community building perfectly. For me, it would provide an opportunity to unplug; a chance to learn from an entirely different type of experience.

With the farm's wide-open vision and my lack of long-term interest in farming, I wasn't sure how to think about or explain this experience, but I knew it could be a valuable piece of my education.

The shift from an office to a farm could be the foundation for seeing the world from another vantage point, and it would give me the space to be thoughtful and inquisitive about what I was learning, what I was doing, and why.

I decided to ask others to join me for a weeklong trip and sent out personal invitations. Two friends jumped on board. Both incredible photographers, Dan Kelleghan and Grant Legan are bright, passionate, and love life; they were the ideal companions for this adventure.

In order to spark conversation and reflection on work, learning, and life, while still giving Dan and Grant space to enjoy the farm and practice their craft, we centered our time at La Choza around these five elements:

READ: I brought a wide range of books from creative thinking and business plan development to personal memoirs and reflection.

There were times where we would go for hours without talking, each person with a different book in our hands. Then inevitably someone would read a line or ask a question, launching deep and meaningful discussions.

WRITE: Stretching butcher paper across a big table, we drew timelines dividing our lives into three parts: past, present, and future.

We wrote down childhood memories, significant moments, successes, and failures. We examined every current idea, relationship, responsibility, or challenge. And with the context of our past and present in mind, we wrote about our future hopes and goals.

OBSERVE: We spent time learning about Costa Rican culture, farm life, the local environment, and what Mariah was doing at La Choza.

CREATE: Being in Costa Rica gave Dan and Grant a fresh palette for their photography and video. They spent time in this setting practicing, creating, and exploring.

WORK: We also had the opportunity to help with a few projects on the farm; fixing things around the house, helping in the garden, and painting one of the buildings on the property.

WORDS OF WISDOM

When we first arrived in Costa Rica, Mariah greeted us at the airport and we crammed into a yellow Land Rover to pick up supplies before a three-hour journey by bus into the mountains where the farm is located.

WOW. THAT MUST HAVE TAKEN A LOT OF TIME.

The following day we met Solin Garcia Sanchez, La Choza's land manager who oversees the farm, trails, and land restoration. He thought we were an odd bunch, which encouraged a good dose of humor and a few pranks that were an unexpected highlight of the trip.

We spent hours with Mariah and Solin as they showed us around the land and shared the team's vision for a fully-sustainable farm — one that would provide food, energy, and material for La Choza while positively impacting the surrounding area.

Solin had spent months learning the best way to plant and grow jatropha, a plant whose gasses generate biofuels. It was extensive and trying work, but he was proud of his efforts and how far the land had come.

As he explained the months of work that had gone into this project, Dan said in passing, "Wow. That must have taken a lot of time."

The reply came, "Yes. Lots of time. All good things take time."

Softly spoken, yet full of wisdom, Solin's words emerged as a theme for our time in Costa Rica.

START PLANTING

Growing anything is challenging and our desire for results can leave us wanting to rush.

But the best type of growth isn't rushed against its nature. It is given time to grow on its own. The only things we can do are prepare, work through the changes, and stay patient for good things to come.

At La Choza, Dan, Grant, Mariah and I took these lessons and applied them to our next steps — writing and sharing the small but necessary tasks to see our careers and our relationships grow well over the following months. We came to understand that none of this would be easy and all of it would take time.

With eight months left in the project and a mountain of ideas, the lesson was a welcomed reminder. I believed in what I was creating and came to realize that much time would have to pass and much effort be expended before the true value of this year would surface.

Each of us are amidst something that needs to grow or change.

Start planting today.

It's going to take time, but that's ok. All good things do.

CONNECT SMALL FARMS WITH BIG APPETITES

TALL TODD JONES
CHICAGO, IL * USA

⌃

When I rode my bike across the country I learned grit, determination, and persistence. So when I decided to start my own business last year — a web-enabled marketplace for locally grown food — I thought that the lessons learned from my cross-country journey would provide me with the exact skill set I would need to succeed.

Boy was I wrong. The same sort of thinking that got me over the never-ending hills of upstate New York proved to be a liability while trying to get a product out the door. I was being bullheaded when I needed to be flexible. I was so mesmerized by the big picture that I didn't pay attention to any of the smaller, simpler solutions along the way. Instead of building a technically complex platform that supports the independent activities of thousands of buyers and sellers, why not get started with a spreadsheet and a cell phone? It seems laughably simple in hindsight, and I only stumbled upon the opportunity when I suggested to someone else that they do the same. Who'd have thunk?

USE ART TO CREATE A
SUSTAINABLE BUSINESS
THAT WILL HELP
OTHERS CREATE THEIR
OWN BUSINESSES &
PURSUE THEIR DREAMS

ALEXANDER CATEDRAL
GROVE CITY, PA * USA

START A BUSINESS &
WORK WITH COMMUNITY
DEVELOPMENT
ORGANIZATIONS TO MAKE
GROVE CITY ONE OF THE
COOLEST SMALL TOWNS
IN AMERICA

KANSAS CITY
MO
USA

GROVE CITY
PA
USA

START A SMALL DESIGN
& BUILD COMPANY
TO MAKE INDUSTRIAL
MODERN FURNITURE
FROM SALVAGED WOOD
& LEND A PORTION
OF THE PROFITS TO
ENTREPRENEURS IN
DEVELOPING COUNTRIES

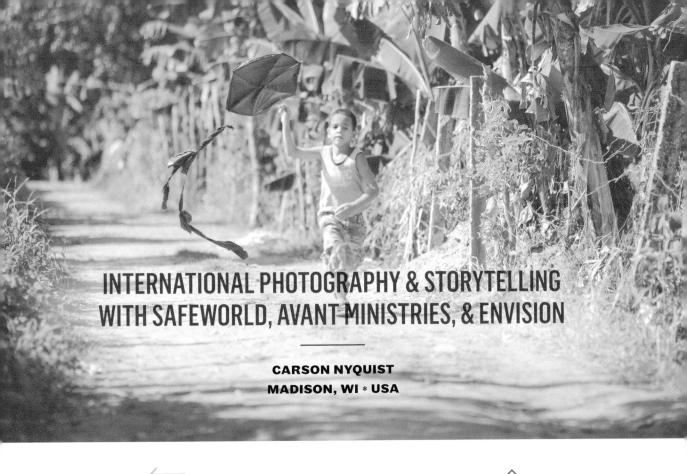

INTERNATIONAL PHOTOGRAPHY & STORYTELLING WITH SAFEWORLD, AVANT MINISTRIES, & ENVISION

CARSON NYQUIST
MADISON, WI * USA

While I wasn't exactly sure what to expect when I committed to The Leap Year Project, what I did know was that I wanted to pursue something I loved, while making a difference at the same time. My mission was twofold: to design and build unique furniture and wooden goods, while doing the most good with our profits and resources. Every piece of wood we use to create our products is special. Each knot, nail hole, defect, and imperfection has a story to tell. We believe these imperfections make each piece perfect and should be celebrated. Not only does this hold true for the wood that we use, but it's also true for each and every life we wish to impact. Every loan we make through Kiva helps a real person with a real need. Each person is special, imperfect, and has a story to tell.

To date, we have made loans to entrepreneurs in Rwanda, Sierra Leone, Paraguay, Palestine, Ukraine, Kenya, Ghana, Guatemala, Honduras, Cambodia, Bolivia, South Sudan, and Armenia.

Being young and inexperienced in photography, I sure didn't have a lot to offer. So I began by looking for ways I could encourage, help, or support people who had helped me. While my contribution was small at first, it was a great mindset to have.

As my opportunities grew, so did my skills, which gave me more chances to thank those who've helped me. One of those opportunities came about when a friend needed a documentary project for his non-profit.

My small steps eventually gave me the abilities and time to produce a film for them, pro bono. In the end, we're all learners. We're all seeking to grow. So, be shameless about it and find ways to benefit others. Who knows where that will take you?

LEARNING TO FAIL

COMMON → MADE
BOULDER, CO

MY WHOLE LIFE, I'VE BEEN THE FIRST ONE TO GIVE CRAZY IDEAS A WHIRL.

I JUMP IN HEADFIRST BUT, DESPITE MY BEST EFFORTS, SOMETIMES THINGS JUST DON'T WORK OUT.

When I began The Leap Year Project, I knew failure was a possibility — it is with any risky, new adventure. But even as I tried to steel myself against this potential disappointment, my ideas and my hopes grew more lofty every day.

Months before, a friend had offered some great advice about the project, including a suggestion that I try to connect with Alex Bogusky, based on his success in the areas I was exploring.

I went home, began researching, and quickly became aware of just how influential Alex Bogusky and his projects have been in the world of advertising and social entrepreneurship.

"There's no way he'll give me the time of day," I thought to myself.

I was mistaken, but as the month unfolded, my up-and-down journey challenged my idea of success and taught me about the many shapes and forms of failure.

LEARNING TO FAIL, AND REDEFINING THAT FAILURE, BECAME MY MOST IMPORTANT LESSON IN MAY.

A COMMON THREAD

The connection came during my time at Threadless. Jake Nickell had mentioned he and Alex were friends and had even collaborated on a t-shirt for Alex's social good agency, COMMON.

Jake generously offered to make an introduction, and that began a series of conversations with one of Alex's partners, Carmel Hagen.

By this point, I was learning to be bold in describing The Leap Year Project. I had been told "no" by so many people that I knew what not to say. I tried to explain to Alex and Carmel how valuable a student and creative helper could be, and they agreed to let me join their team in May.

COMMON was based in Boulder. I had never been there, I didn't know anyone, nor did I have the resources to afford lodging. Thankfully, a chance meeting with a friend of a friend named Amber started me off on the right foot before I left Chicago. Amber Rae, a blooming entrepreneur and writer, was amidst a busy season and needed some interior design help. She offered to let me exchange my design eye and thrifting skills for a month's rent and I accepted.

As I boarded the plane, I knew that a chance to work with Alex and COMMON was an amazing opportunity, but this particular month would prove to be full of challenges.

THE BEST DAMN BURRITO

Upon landing in Denver, I took the next bus to a Boulder coffee shop to meet with Carmel. COMMON, the company I was supposed to apprentice with, had just entered a time of unexpected major change, and she and I began discussing how this would impact my time there.

Carmel was afraid my role would fall through the cracks because of the changes. I told her I'd be free to help in any way, and that

I could find something to do. She wanted to help make sure the month was valuable for me, but neither of us were sure at this point if that was actually possible.

Exhausted from a long day of travel, I headed to a nearby burrito joint with a slew of questions running through my mind. I walked to the counter with all my luggage in hand and announced that I was new in town and wanted the best damn burrito they had. They laughed and served me exactly what I asked for.

A guy in his late twenties overheard I was new and invited me to sit with him. His name was Pete McBride, and he told me he had quit his job and set out to tour the country, live on as little as possible, explore new running trails, and push himself physically and mentally.

We shared stories from our adventures, hopes of where we might go, and how to continue our journeys well. Our interaction may have been brief, but random meetings like this one with Pete lifted my spirits and became some of the best moments of the year.

I was encouraged, but still facing a difficult month ahead. While boldness and inspiration were moving my leap forward, they wouldn't necessarily shelter me from uncertainty, or even failure.

FAILURE IN MY OWN MIND

Despite the initial uncertainty following my meeting with Carmel, I found a place to start. I began by helping organize an upcoming event where individuals would have the opportunity to present their ideas for social innovation to the COMMON team.

My role was to help narrow the applicants down to the top eight. Sifting through the many ideas was inspiring, but that project didn't require my full time and energy. I was lacking direction; Carmel had flown to New York for a project, Bogusky was busy, and I was stuck.

EVERY GOOD STORY INVOLVES SOME SORT OF STRUGGLE.

MAY 11

@victorsaad: Another meal w/ a complete stranger who turned out to be an amazing guy. Do what's right, and often you'll meet the right people.

MAR 30

"Beware the lollipop of mediocrity. Lick it once and you suck forever." — things I hear in the office.

Lonely, broke, and riding a girl's bike to pick up groceries, I began questioning whether I should have come. So far, every other month had worked out so well, but this one seemed to be crumbling beneath me.

I doubted my move to Boulder and questioned whether this entire year would ever be considered valuable.

Although I was doing my best to keep busy and had even made a couple of friends, I was still feeling somewhat alone. Often, I'd find myself with too much time; getting lost in my thoughts, staying up late writing, pondering, and feeling as though May's leap was a giant failure.

A LONG-AWAITED CONVERSATION

On my twelfth day in Boulder, Alex and I finally sat down for our first real chat. I was nervous, but after a few questions, we launched into an incredible two-hour conversation ranging from design and education to faith and family.

In the end, Alex invited me to finish my month working with MADE, a close friend's start-up agency focused on advertising and selling the best American-made products on the market.

He pointed me to their office, and a few hours later I was sitting at a desk with several brilliant, big-hearted people.

The following days were full. I arrived early, left late, and tried to help in any way possible, working with the team to explore target audiences and potential partners. More importantly, I quickly became part of the team — sharing laughs, hearing stories, understanding their passion for this new company, and working in the trenches together toward something meaningful.

YOU MIGHT NOT FEEL LIKE YOU'RE GETTING ANYWHERE, BUT KEEP GOING.

"NO ONE KNOWS WHAT THEY'RE DOING, ANYWAY."

During one of my chats with Alex, we discussed some of the lessons he had learned during his twenties.

The biggest lesson, he said, was that most people simply build up their experiences to the point where they have failed so much that they intuitively know what to do and what not to do next. No one knows what they're doing, anyway.

A certain confidence comes with this realization; that we're all just figuring things out as we go, that you're in the same spot as everyone else. You might not feel like you're getting anywhere, but keep going.

Success doesn't come from having all of the answers at the beginning — rather, the people who succeed are the ones who know that they'll have to work through the challenges and continue anyway.

WHAT FAILURE TAUGHT ME

During my first few weeks in Boulder, I was sure that I was failing, falling through the cracks. In the end, I was able to make a small impact on a team with a meaningful mission.

Failure taught me to move slowly, to consider my next steps carefully, and not to compare my own shortcomings to those of others.

Failure reminded me that success doesn't come without effort. Every good story involves some sort of struggle.

Failure taught me to be flexible. If you're going to try something new, it will never go exactly as planned. Be prepared to roll with the changes.

But most importantly, I learned that you're not a failure if you've tried something new. Sure, it may not always turn out as you imagined, but failure is not the end...

...it's just the beginning.

LAUNCH A COMPANY THAT SELLS HEIRLOOM QUALITY WOODEN TOYS

CHRIS HUIZENGA
CHICAGO, IL * USA

NOBLE

Our initial launch wasn't successful; what I've learned is that it is essential to pivot. Never back up, never quit — pivot. And some of the values touted early on may also have to pivot based on what realities finally materialize.

This is as much about teaching as it is learning, and sometimes those two things happen in tandem.

What's next? Bringing along the right people for the next leg of the ride and exploring the best ways to design, source, and produce quality toys.

GO ON A SHORT-TERM MISSION TO TEACH MUSIC & ART IN THE DOMINICAN REPBUBLIC

ELIZABETH SORENSON
BATAVIA, IL * USA

In January of 2012, my husband, John, went on his second service trip to Nicaragua. Nearly 200 workers served 4,500 people in just a few days. Some did medical and dental work, others helped roof a school "auditorium", and helped finish a one-room church and one-room pastor's house.

John wanted me to see the area, buildings, and meet the pastor of this village; so we flew down there the next month. It was a difficult leap for me, but John was so enthusiastic about it that I wanted to go. It quickly became obvious to me that I didn't fit. I loved the people but was just too extremely far out of all my comfort zones. There isn't a garbage or septic system in the city, so I suddenly recognized that I have a bit of germaphobia in me. My over-65-year-old knees don't work well and one is replaced. I was very afraid of walking on the torn-up, cobblestone, uneven surfaces, with random holes every 20-50 feet.

The trip was so stressful that, upon returning home, I broke out into an awful case of the shingles. Still, we made plans to go on a second trip; this time to the home of some friends in the Dominican Republic to help with their mission work. So in early March, we took off again so I could teach and John could help do repairs at their school.

My husband somehow rebuilt a lot of broken desks, repaired chalkboards, refinished two teacher desks, and helped with an upcoming business conference. I taught music and art to pre-k through 6th grade. I had been apprehensive about this, but the love and joy flowing out of the kids, and knowing that God had given me ideas of what to teach was the fuel I needed for the week. I finished up the teaching on the very day I broke out into a second case of shingles, which turned out to be the most painful thing I've ever felt. (Note: I've had natural childbirth and knee replacement, so I can speak to this).

My favorite part of the teaching last year was starting the first Dominican Kazoo Band. The kids were all given kazoos and we blasted a song called "1000 Kazoos" on the CD player. The 80 kids danced, giggled, and made the surrounding roosters crow. We're currently packing for another trip in a couple of weeks...complete with more kazoos, and this time, drumsticks too! Sounds more like a setup for headaches instead of shingles.

DRAFT MY FIRST NON-FICTION BOOK ABOUT BALANCING LIFE BETWEEN BEING A WIFE, MOMMA, & GROWING MORE IN MY FAITH

CAMILLE HO
MAIDSTONE, KENT ∗ ENGLAND

EXPLORE HOW TO USE MY BUSINESS SKILLS & GLOBAL EXPERIENCES TO MAKE THE WORLD A BETTER PLACE

MUFFADAL SAYLAWALA
CHICAGO, IL ∗ USA

The biggest challenge I've faced in taking this leap is failure and defeat. I've tried a few different things, put my all into them, and really thought they would work; but they didn't. The most difficult thing I've dealt with is having the fortitude to keep going and not let the failures and the setbacks bring me down.

It's not about the end destination; all the fun and learning really happens on the way there.

I'm not entirely sure what's in store for me next and I love that.

←

TAKE CONTROL OF MY CAREER TO BE HAPPIER & MAKE MORE OF AN IMPACT FOR GOOD THROUGH DESIGN

ALISON KUCZWARA
CHICAGO, IL * USA

After about 3.5 years at a small marketing firm, a perfect storm occurred where I realized that I wasn't being creatively challenged, inspired or helping others for the greater good. It all led to an unfortunate feeling of losing passion in the career path I chose.

As I was contemplating what to do, a best friend reminded me that, "it's not that you don't love what you do, you just don't love where you are." This truly struck home with me.

I knew that in order to keep doing design in some capacity five years from now, I'd have to leave my current position. "But leave a full time steady gig in this recession?!?!" said EVERYONE. Yes. Doing things on my own — as scary as it felt — was better than losing passion in something I truly love.

The biggest challenge came right when I was ready to quit. It became apparent that I would need surgery on my wrist. After a few days of sadness and lots of harsh thoughts towards my wrist, I decided to not let it stand in my way.

I put my notice in anyway and planned for surgery. After a couple days of recovery, I started learning a few tricks to cheat my doctor's orders and I even learned how to brush my teeth with my left hand! More importantly, I learned it feels much better to see what can be accomplished than to feel regret for not taking chances.

Since taking this chance I've been able to contribute to good causes such as a Chicago non-profit helping young refugee girls, a non-profit in Miami that provides speech therapy for autistic children, and brand a company that pairs large corporations with charities and schools to donate to.

Next up will be pursuing more personal projects that get me away from the computer, while continuing to do design for fantastic people.

CREATING SPACE

—

NBBJ
SEATTLE, WA

GROWTH
REQUIRES
SPACE

GROWTH REQUIRES SPACE; SPACE TO BREATHE, TO LEARN, TO EXPLORE.

SOMETIMES WE HAVE TO INTENTIONALLY CREATE THAT SPACE FOR OURSELVES. BUT SOMETIMES IT IS CREATED FOR US, THROUGH UNEXPECTED LIFE CHANGE, A NEW OPPORTUNITY, OR THE THOUGHTFUL INTRODUCTION OF A FRIEND.

This was the case in June, when a good friend suggested I connect with Samuel Stubblefield, a generous, brilliant designer and architect in Seattle.

Working for a renowned architecture firm, NBBJ, Sam specializes in Experiential and Environmental Design; using art and technology as a means to improve the experience of spaces within a community.

Fascinated by Sam's work, I reached out and we soon began discussing his passion for using space to foster community and conversation. During our phone calls, I began to understand why Sam found his work so valuable and knew I wanted to spend time learning from him.

Finally, Sam told me, "Victor, just find a month where you can spend time working with me in Seattle. We'll find something worthwhile for you to do. I'm sure of it."

MEETING SAM

I knew from the moment Sam picked me up from Sea-Tac airport that June's leap would be very different from May's. Having found out that I had no place to stay, Sam invited me to live with him, and within the first two days, we had planned our entire time together.

We placed two large sheets of butcher paper on the wall; one for his ideas, dreams, and projects, and one for mine. Using different colored markers, we wrote down anything and everything we hoped to create, launch, or improve, and then thought through how we could help each other.

Those two sheets remained on the wall for the rest of our time together and we checked back almost daily.

Coming to Seattle provided space for me to see, explore, and learn, and with Sam's help, this idea of creating space not only became my practice, but my field of study for the entire month.

OFFICE SPACE

On the third day, Sam took me to his office. NBBJ has offices around the world sectioned into teams or 'studios,' each with a specific number and a specialized focus. Studio 05 focused primarily on healthcare buildings. Studio 41 focused on corporate offices.

Sam works with Studio 07, the in-house design firm. Their focus revolves around exploring how a space would be experienced, navigated, and remembered using graphic and interior design, spatial layout, wayfinding, and integrated digital graphics.

As Sam introduced me to the team and showed me the projects, I was blown away.

I never knew how extensive and important spatial design could be. We began discussing how, even though our world is becoming increasingly digital, we will always live and move and work in physical spaces; each of which has an opportunity to inform, inspire, serve, and connect people.

"Sam! This is incredible. I've never thought about architecture in this way," I said excitedly. "But, how in the world can I be helpful?"

Sam told me he had made a case for me to actually join NBBJ as a paid apprentice for the remainder of the month. Now, I just needed to present some of my past work and what I could do for the team.

"You've got two hours. Prepare a presentation and convince the team why you should be here."

All I had to go on were my previous conversations with Sam and the team, including one where he mentioned Studio 07's need to define and explain their work to the rest of the firm.

Oftentimes, he explained, the studio was viewed as just a graphics department, which was only one part of their role. I used this need as the foundation for my presentation, explaining how I could help refresh their image in order to give them the space to continue doing innovative work.

It's not everyday that a kid shows up at your office as a drop-in apprentice willing to help. Curious and intrigued, they gave me some feedback on my ideas, and then gave me the job.

DESIGNING SPACE

During the day, I was working on rebranding Studio 07 within the overall firm. At night, I researched Experience Design. Sam would brainstorm with me and challenge me on every idea, and he recommended good books and authors to check out from their in-house library.

Rebranding required an inquisitive approach. After interviewing each member of the team to find out how they thought about their own department, I researched how the other departments

normally interacted with Studio 07 and identified key people in each one. I met with each person individually, and by asking questions and listening, I was able to learn everything I needed to know.

Along the way, the marketing department heard what I was doing and invited me to present to their team.

I spent late nights tightening my presentation. I wanted to share the insight I had gained in a helpful way, so with Sam's help, I created a brief write-up and presentation on behalf of Studio 07, explaining who they are and what they do.

This informative one-page document gave the Studio 07 team a starting point and the vocabulary for sharing the work they do and what they value.

The ideas and thoughts behind my proposal were there inside the Studio 07 teammates the whole time, all we needed was time to explore — all we needed was a little space.

SPACE IS AN OPPORTUNITY

In every aspect of our lives, we are faced with decisions regarding space. Will we fill it, or leave it open? What will we place on our walls? How will we organize our rooms?

Each of these questions requires an answer, and each answer carries a consequence.

The way we arrange physical space dictates how we move and interact, what we see, how we process, and how we impact the people around us.

This same idea applies to time.

If we decide to fill every moment, we leave little room to attempt something new, little time to focus on the things we are already working on.

I think this is why The Leap Year Project needs to exist. It's an invitation to establish a new rhythm of creating space, and to work together — you, me, and the wide-eyed person next to us — to claim that space, and use it together to refocus on what matters most.

During my time with Sam, I learned that a leap can provide initial space to grow, but it's only the first step. This is not a one-time task, but an intentional process that we must engage every day; a decision to design our lives in a way that provides the space and time to work, learn, explore, and grow.

JUN 25

@victorsaad: 6 months. 10 lessons. (...and 6 months to go)

Create ———— .

LAUNCH THE WORLD'S FIRST
AUGMENTED REALITY PUBLIC
ART PLATFORM

SEATTLE
WA
USA

There are so many people that haven't been connected to a growing genre of art. We're all missing out — society and the artists. We need to design and build physical pedestals for digital sculptures to be displayed on. I figured I could help.

Jumping into something that doesn't exist takes some amount of child-like openness and adult-like craziness. There have been difficulties along the way. At some point I told myself, "Look, you're never going to regret taking some time off to focus on this. Go figure it out." After making that decision, things happened. I knew the two ingredients were time and focus. I made some decisive cuts to existing projects, social obligations, other startup prospects and a few great opportunities.

At first, the methodical focus was oriented around learning. Daunting technical hurdles of learning how to use this emerging technology, learning to code, learning an entirely new language of the Augmented Reality ethos. Some long weekends and late nights later, there sat in front of me a working prototype. I knew nothing about this type of technology just a few months before. Now I was able to hang in a conversation with some of the best people in the field. Interesting what a little focus and time will do. That said, my house is a wreck.

OPEN A NEW CAFE & MARKETPLACE FOCUSED ON THOUGHTFUL FOOD & INTENTIONAL SPACE

→

∧

The goal was to create an environment that feels comfortable, where the music sets the tone and the food welcomes conversation and celebration.

One of the most beautiful things about opening a local cafe and coffee shop is the numerous people that you get to meet. Local merchants, neighbors, and friends of friends walk through the door every day and it is a joy to learn their names and their story.

We set out to create a space where the community could connect and belong, and that's what we're doing.

GLEN ELLYN
IL
USA

It had already been months into the planning. My mind was made up and my will was set. I was about to take the summer to cross the country of Canada — on a bicycle — by myself.

This was going to push my limits, push my comfort zone, and expand it too. For the first time in my life I was NOT going to know where I would be sleeping or exactly how I was going to get from point A to point B. So many questions, so many challenges, all of which needed answers.

And so began my trek, from my beloved hometown city of Dallas TX to a never before seen part of the country. At first, it seemed as if the ride would never end, not that I wanted it to, it's just that I was realizing how big of an undertaking the adventure was. Ontario, Manitoba, Saskatchewan, Alberta, and onwards. The feeling of "nothing can stop me now" had been fully absorbed.

Each day was truly a new day in every sense. I had choices, and each one of them was mine. That was freedom.

I arrived in Calgary almost 2 months after the start of my ride. It had been a hard, cold, wet day, and also one of the longest. This was the finish line.

As some of the folk back home would do, I cried a mighty 'yee-haw!'

CYCLING ACROSS CANADA

JUAN PABLO TABOADA
DALLAS, TX * USA

FINALLY MOVING TO AUSTIN

KATHRYN REILLY
AUSTIN, TX * USA

SPEND 15 MINUTES EVERY MORNING IN QUIET TIME

**KATHLEEN LINCOLN
DELAVAN, WI, * USA**

I wanted to develop this habit to quiet my spirit from the noise and urgency of daily life. It was my hope that this simple act would increase focus and energy.

It wasn't always easy to carve this time out of my day. There were times when a warm bed urged me to hit the snooze instead of getting up. Other times, I awoke and demands rushed at me. But there were wonderful days when I did go to that quiet place, both in my house and in my heart, and found myself refreshed.

$\leftarrow$

$\leftarrow$

IMPROVE THE HEALTH OF MY COMMUNITY BY HELPING THEM THROUGH EDUCATION & HABIT CHANGE

**ASHLEY FLITTER
MINNESOTA • USA**

After getting into the greatest shape of my life and feeling the best I'd ever felt, I decided that I wanted to share that feeling with others.

I started a wellness club at work and implemented initiatives such as Walking Warriors, a group that takes 10-minute walks every other day during their breaks, and completes wellness challenges. I had a great response from people within my company and throughout the year.

Soon, many people — both family and friends — came to me for personal health advice and tips.

I began seeing people transform their habits right in front of my eyes.

HAPPY ARE THOSE WHO DREAM DREAMS AND ARE READY TO PAY THE PRICE TO MAKE THEM COME TRUE.

—Cardinal Suenens

Throughout the year, we encouraged Leapers to tell their stories online. They shared their ups and downs through Twitter, Facebook, blogs, and photographs. Stories from around the world were collected; some made us laugh, some inspired us, some moved us to tears.

But they were all connected by one thing — a hashtag attached to their updates: #LYProject

#1

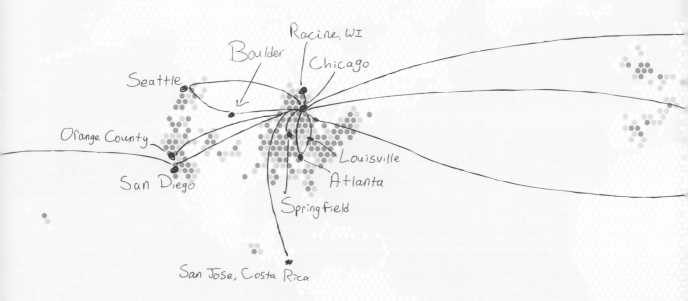

Racine, WI

Boulder

Chicago

Seattle

Orange County

San Diego

Louisville

Atlanta

Springfield

San Jose, Costa Rica

VICTOR'S LEAP **29** **FLIGHTS** 58,31

SEIZE
THE
YEAR

247
LEAPERS

Istanbul

Beijing

Cairo

COUNTRIES

Shanghai

216

MILES 216 DAYS ON THE ROAD

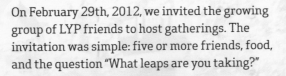

On February 29th, 2012, we invited the growing group of LYP friends to host gatherings. The invitation was simple: five or more friends, food, and the question "What leaps are you taking?"

All of us different, yet bound by our hopes, met to share how we were working to create positive change in our lives, communities, and our world.

LEAPDAY MEETUPS

CHICAGO, IL + KYOTO, JAPAN + LOS ANGELES, CA + HOUSTON, TX + PARIS, FRANCE

SEATTLE, WA + DENVER, CO + SOUDERTON, PA + LAS CRUCES, NM + KARLSRUHE, GERMANY

Throughout the year, we came across some great Leap Quotes. So we invited a few designers to create posters that would inspire others who were on the brink of something great.

Download these as iPhone and iPad backgrounds at www.LeapYearProject.org.

[THIS PAGE] DESIGN Debbie Millman QUOTE Daniel Burnham

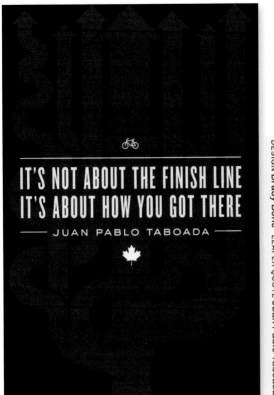

IT'S NOT ABOUT THE FINISH LINE
IT'S ABOUT HOW YOU GOT THERE
— JUAN PABLO TABOADA —

DESIGN Brady Bone   LEAPER QUOTE Juan Pablo Taboada

DESIGN Justin Ahrens   LEAPER QUOTE Justin Ahrens

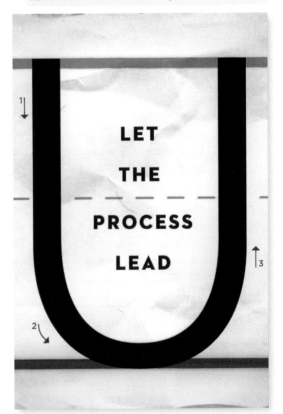

LET
THE

PROCESS

LEAD

THE LEAPYEAR PROJECT

DESIGN Hendrika Makilya   LEAPER QUOTE Tristan Pollock

PERSPECTIVE

———

HOME
CHICAGO, IL

VANTAGE

THE FIRST TIME I FLEW IN AN AIRPLANE, I WAS IN MIDDLE SCHOOL.

MY PARENTS HAD DECIDED TO TAKE A FAMILY TRIP TO LAS VEGAS, AND WHILE THEY LOVED THE INCREDIBLE SHOWS, SHINY LIGHTS, AND GLASS PYRAMIDS, TO ME, NOTHING WAS MORE SPECTACULAR THAN THE FLIGHT.

I remember bouncing through the terminals, pointing and shouting with joy at every detail. As we boarded, I had to contain the odd combination of brewing fear and billowing excitement welling up inside me. I waddled onto the airplane, took the window seat that my mother gladly offered, and strapped into my new cockpit.

Then the magic happened. We — became — airborne.

Everything that was once large and daunting became tiny and manageable. I could somehow see both the airport and my neighborhood. As we rose, people became specks and cars became ants. The roads shrunk, miles turned to inches, and buildings flattened into two dimensions.

For the first time, I saw the world from a new vantage point. And that new perspective changed the way I saw and thought about everything moving forward.

I've taken countless flights since then — especially during this project. In fact, by the time July hit I had stayed in six cities, worked for four companies, and slept on more couches than I have fingers and toes.

I WAS SPENT.

As I prepared for the second half of the year, my best friend, Tyler Savage, strongly suggested taking a month to rest and 'gain perspective.' The constant movement hadn't allowed any space for me to rest or reflect. I needed a different vantage point, and he knew it.

97

REST AND PERSPECTIVE ARE OFTEN ELUSIVE

BALANCING PERSPECTIVE

Taking time to gain perspective felt like losing momentum. Did I really have the time? At this point, The Leap Year Project had become a balancing act; simultaneously investing in my apprenticeship, wherever I happened to be, while also encouraging the community side of the project and arranging experiences for the rest of the year.

To continue at this pace, I needed to learn how to better incorporate rest into my daily life, so I turned to my good friend and mentor, Iain Boyd.

As the head of human resources at a large, international company, Iain, a tall, dapper Scottish man with silver hair and wise wrinkles has had to work to establish a healthy balance between his personal and professional life.

Winsome and interesting, he loves to cook, read, travel, and has an incredible talent for interior design.

Iain had already been involved as a mentor prior to The Leap Year Project, so it was a natural fit for me to spend time with him at his home in Wisconsin. We took walks, went for runs, cooked meals, and spent hours talking about both life and work.

But no matter how hard I drilled into my agenda with questions, tasks, and ideas, he would always turn the conversation back to matters of the head and heart. Each of his questions would linger for hours as they sparked further thoughts and stories.

As part of these introspective and in-depth discussions, Iain often encouraged me to reflect on how I was growing wiser; pushing me to list the things I was doing well: a tenacious work ethic, a boyish curiosity, a thick skin, a soft heart, an empowering spirit.

It was a valuable reminder, and one I would lean on heavily throughout the year.

PEOPLE AS PROFESSORS

During my time with Iain, we talked about how to continue sitting across from people and giving them a 'podium' in my life — to be reminded of the value in asking questions, listening to stories, and learning from different points of view.

I began setting up meetings with an array of friends, leaders, and mentors; giving each of them an update on the project and asking them to speak into it. I wanted to give them permission and space to teach, correct, or encourage.

These interactions didn't result in profound changes, but by stepping away from a structured apprenticeship and seeking new insight, I was able to see holes in the project I hadn't before. Taking the time to listen and look at the project through the eyes of others helped me approach the following months with fresh energy.

LOOKING AHEAD

Though it was only July, nearly every conversation included the question, "So, what's next for you after this year?"

I understood the question, but I hated it.

Perhaps I was scared because I was unsure of what was next. Or perhaps I was more concerned with the coming months than the end of the year. Either way, the question challenged me.

Towards the beginning of the year, Jake from Threadless had planted the idea in my mind that my program would make an incredible school — one that was based on experiences over the course of a year. Unsure of how to actually make that happen, I pushed the idea to the back of my mind, but in July, it resurfaced and I began putting all of the ideas on paper.

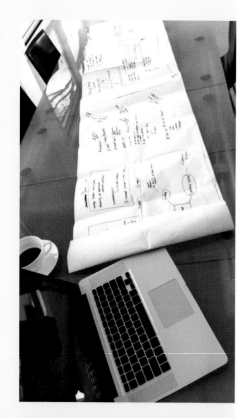

I was back to wondering if I should stop The Leap Year Project early; this time to jump in with both feet and start creating the school. I toyed with the idea. Staying in one city and building a team was enticing, but in the end, I knew I had a community of friends, donors, mentors, and Leapers who expected me to finish.

HOME UNBOUND

Planning ahead, I realized I would be spending most, if not all, of the next five months outside of Chicago. I couldn't really justify the cost of rent, so I began the difficult process of purging my belongings. By the end, the only things I had left to my name fit inside a roller bag and a backpack; a feeling that was both liberating and terrifying.

My mind was packed with questions. "Should I really move forward? Is this worth it? Am I inching towards a vagabond life?"

Those thoughts kept me up at night and forced me to examine my idea of home.

In these moments, both Tyler and Iain reminded me that 'home' is often more than a physical space. They pushed me to identify and seek out things that made me feel most at home no matter where I was.

That question, "What makes you feel at home?" became an ongoing conversation among friends, and I discovered those things as I moved around: hummus and pita, a heavy blanket, good music, sharing stories over a good meal, phone calls with friends, and any opportunity to view an expanse of land or water.

With that in mind, it was time to gather my belongings, give away a few final items, and pack for the journey.

HERE AND NOW

Rest and perspective are often elusive. Most of us understand their importance, but our relationships, responsibilities, and of course, pursuing our dreams, tend to fill up our schedules. It's hard to find margin because we constantly have so much going on.

The time I set aside during the month of July was necessary. I was able to evaluate where I was headed for the second half of the year and even beyond. It was from then on that the school idea really started to evolve and grow in my mind as I thought about the future.

But as the end of the month approached, I had to put aside my grand ideas of what would come post-project to get back to the next few months' experiences. In fact, during one of my 'perspective conversations,' a friend snapped his fingers and said:

"Why are you thinking so much about January? It sounds like it's time for you to work on August."

It was a healthy reminder.

There is an obvious tension between what's here now and what's to come, especially when you're so focused on change. Carving out moments or seasons for rest and perspective doesn't mean forgetting about your present challenge.

Instead, it's like strapping into an airplane and getting a sky-high view of your surroundings, an opportunity to turn off the demands of your daily routine and take a fresh look at your trajectory. Eventually you'll land, and when you do, you'll have a better idea of where you are, how far you've come, and why it's so important that you keep going.

Roller bag in hand, I boarded a plane once more.

Next stop, San Diego.

JUL 03

@victorsaad: Hmmm...I'm going to turn into the Egyptian Leonardo DiCaprio if this continues. #catchmeifyoucan

LAUNCH A CINEMATOGRAPHY BUSINESS, RE-INSTILLING THE DESIRE TO LEARN THE CRAFT OF IMAGE & FILMMAKING

KEVIN VON QUALEN
DENVER, CO * USA

LEAVE THE SAFETY OF A STABLE TEACHING JOB TO BE A TEACHER-ARTIST IN A NEW THEATRE COMPANY

Using film causes us to be intentional about what we are shooting, as it can be expensive. And that intentionality in our art naturally causes us to see differently, and then better create. Image manipulation has become so common that we are now trained to think that the unattainable figures on magazines are normal. We've also lost the ability to see the beauty in growing old. Shooting film feels permanent in a disposable culture, and it teaches us to see beauty in the imperfections.

The perspective I've learned about myself is that I'm more risk averse than I thought. I've learned that choosing what I believe in and then moving forward gains more respect than mimicking others. I've learned that making your own path is the best marketing tool as people gravitate to what is different and innovative. I've also learned that fear is the best compass.

BRISBANE
QLD
AUSTRALIA

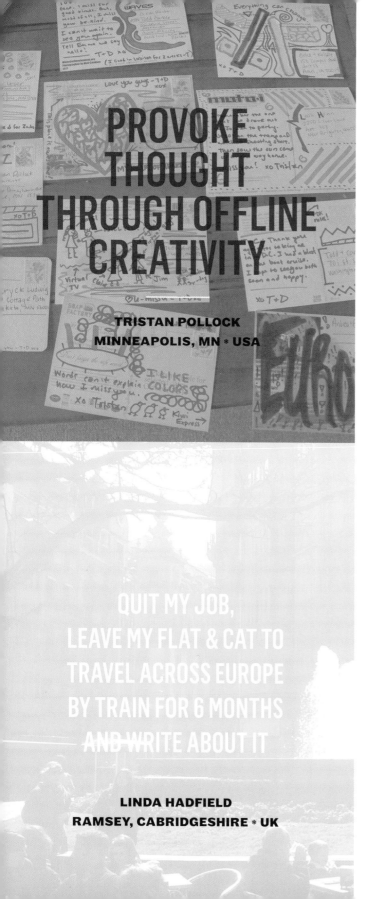

PROVOKE THOUGHT THROUGH OFFLINE CREATIVITY

TRISTAN POLLOCK
MINNEAPOLIS, MN ∗ USA

QUIT MY JOB, LEAVE MY FLAT & CAT TO TRAVEL ACROSS EUROPE BY TRAIN FOR 6 MONTHS AND WRITE ABOUT IT

LINDA HADFIELD
RAMSEY, CABRIDGESHIRE ∗ UK

I made a commitment to myself to create things with my hands.

Furthermore, my urge to remain extremely loyal to the people who support and drive me keeps me thinking about ways to nurture important relationships instead of letting them flutter and die. With communication technology reaching a critical mass of overload, I knew I needed a new creative outlet to share my feelings, comedy, and to send a little personal "hello" to those I care about.

Enter postcards.

Writing postcards gave me an outlet to create while focusing on those around me, all while provoking little snail mail smiles. Most importantly, those that matter the most know I'm still thinking about them.

←

I traveled over 11,000 miles by train, bus and boat. I stayed with friends, or found lodgings online, rarely knowing exactly where I was going to be more than a day or two in advance. Someone said, "I hope you find what you're looking for." But I didn't know what that was, and it bothered me; until I realised maybe it's better just to keep going and appreciate whatever it is that I do find.

The trip had brought out things in me that I knew were there but other people might not have recognised: I'm happy with my own company, I value my independence, arrivals and departures can be stressful (but the bits in between are wonderful), I can get lost but it's no big deal because I still end up somewhere, and as long as I have a bed for the night, food in my belly and somewhere to go the next day, everything will take care of itself.

The toughest thing I've had to learn is how to be ok with uncertainty. Leaving dear friends, a steady paycheck, and familiar cities has been difficult; but since leaving, I have adopted the ability to be content with where I am and trust I'll find what I need.

Along the way, I hope to gain a sense of what I'm put on Earth to do. I believe this comes primarily from listening and discovering those things that give life and energize. I'm hoping that at some point there will be a moment of, "Yes, that's what I need to do."

SAN FRANCISCO CA USA

A YEAR TO
RECHARGE & REST
THAT TURNED INTO
FOLLOWING MY HEART,
WRITING A BOOK,
A FEW LONG HIKES,
& VISITING MY
ANCESTRAL ROOTS

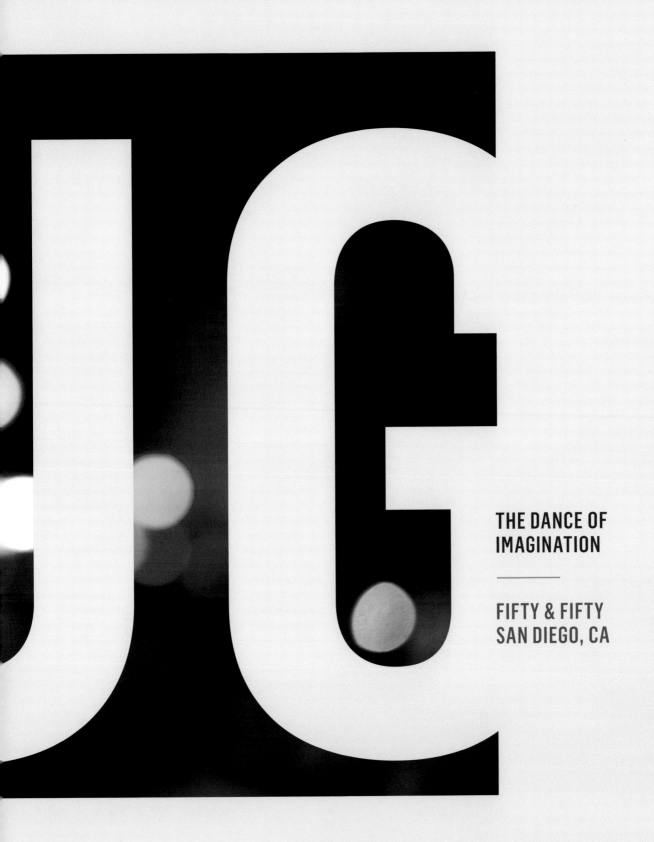

THE DANCE OF
IMAGINATION

FIFTY & FIFTY
SAN DIEGO, CA

PURSUIT

IMAGINATION MOVES. IT DOESN'T STAY STILL.

IT ISN'T EASY TO FIND, WHICH MAKES THAT TRIUMPHANT MOMENT OF DISCOVERY ALL SO SWEET.

For me, The Leap Year Project was a constant pursuit of imagination; a blank slate, waiting to be painted as I explored, learned, and tried to make a difference in the world.

By the time August rolled around, I had the end of the year in sight, and I found myself once again staring at a blank slate. But this time, I needed a new type of imagination.

Beginning a leap requires a certain kind of reckless and optimistic imagination, but to continue leaping requires something more; an imagination fueled by tenacity, intention... and a healthy dose of stubbornness.

It was the first time all year I had three months of experiences lined up ahead of time. July had given me the time and space to see what the finish line could look like and now there was no turning back.

SITUATED IN SAN DIEGO

After snagging the last seat on a standby flight, I landed in San Diego to connect with Ryan Sisson and Bryan Monzon. They worked for Fifty & Fifty, a top-notch web agency focused solely on non-profit organizations and social good companies. Billed as a humanitarian creative studio, and committed to "Engage the world with the worthwhile," Fifty & Fifty was relatively new, but had already been recognized for their notable work.

These guys were good and I was excited to learn from them. But as usual, I didn't know what I would be doing or how I would add value to such a talented team of developers and designers.

Thankfully, since Bryan's roommate had moved out just a few days prior, I at least knew I had a place to stay. Looking back at the project as a whole, it's uncanny how often this happened; how often the perfect solution came at the perfect time, even when I hadn't been able to see it before.

Bryan's home was a ten-mile bike ride from the office, but the San Diego weather was fantastic and being on the bike offered me a substantial amount of time each day to think, process, and take in the sights.

WHO'S YOUR VILLAIN?

Fifty & Fifty was working with incredible organizations engaged in a variety of arenas, from clean water, international aid, and anti-sex trafficking to political action, youth engagement, and education.

Again, I found myself asking the question, "How can I help?" A friend of mine, Dan Portnoy, mentioned a profound idea during one of our phone calls that stirred my imagination:

FIND YOUR VILLAIN

"Everyone needs to find their villain. The bigger the villain, the better the story. This is why everyone hates The Joker in Batman. We all want the good guy to win. So, who, or what, is your villain?"

The villain is the obstacle, the challenge, the impossible situation, the thing with the creepy grin.

I began to hunt for the villain in the office.

Similar to my work in June, I arranged interviews with each team member and began investigating; asking questions about their role, their motivations, their projects, their hopes, and their frustrations.

With each interview, I was able to better understand the office dynamics and the challenges. And as certain themes continued to emerge, I began catching glimpses of the villain.

Spotting it is just the beginning, but it directs the rest of the process; helping you know what to research, who to partner with, and how to keep going when you're stuck.

But naming the villain isn't always easy or straightforward. Sharing what you think it might be and seeking outside perspective is critical. Often, we end up vilifying the wrong things — our competitors, world leaders, small bank accounts, fame — but the villains worth destroying are the ones that hurt, belittle, or divide people.

At Fifty & Fifty, for example, one of the common themes, or villains, was not having a unified story, or a way to share that story. They were working so hard on outside projects that no one had time to develop the agency's own identity. With the villain in mind, I got to work; immersing myself in their story and brand, dissecting copy, brainstorming a new site, and refreshing their social media presence.

As we worked together, I had the unexpected opportunity to help the team plan and launch their first web application — a donation platform for non-profits. The rest of the month, I studied everything I could about existing software and how we could position the new product in a growing market.

AUG 22

@victorsaad: Oh, for the imagination to be set free and the heart be stirred — there is no danger so beautiful...no instance so hopeful.

AUG 10

Tell me...
I forget.
Show me...
I remember.
Involve me...
I understand.

111

IMAGINATION REQUIRES OBSERVATION AND ENDURANCE.

Imagination was necessary for us to move beyond typical jargon and towards creative solutions. We worked together to come up with fun ways to share not only the product's features, but also the story behind it and why it was needed. Their story was becoming more unified and, at the same time, easier to share.

It was hard work, but defeating the villain always is.

SOMETHING DIFFERENT

The team at Fifty & Fifty reinforced for me the importance of stepping away from the computer and refueling your creativity.

Although there was never a shortage of work to keep them busy, they tried to hold realistic office hours rather than burning the midnight oil. And when the work was done, they were surfers, tri-athletes, foodies, and friends.

Viewing work as just one part of their life, the team knew that rest and play gave them energy, and provided a fresh perspective on the job at hand.

Early in the month, the team forced me to close my laptop and join them for a weekend trip to the seaside camping spot Ryan had been saving since February. We packed his trailer with an abundance of food, surfing gear, and supplies, and met the guys for two days of good times and the surprisingly difficult task of wrestling the strange, albino alligator that was my surfboard.

I never managed to surf an entire wave that weekend, but there was something eye-opening about being on the open water and trying something so foreign. Inspired by the sights and humbled by the power of nature, I found myself, my problems, and my workload feeling small — in the best kind of way.

My problems and my workload didn't shrink, they were just put in their place.

The entire month was littered with these types of moments to refuel — most of which revolved around good food, deep conversation, and the occasional bike ride with thousands of people through downtown San Diego.

Every time, I came back refreshed.

IMAGINATION'S PLACE

It's no secret that imagination is valuable. It's what sparks new inventions and fuels great stories. Too often, however, we assume that our imagination is there waiting for us, ready to be turned on at a moment's notice.

It isn't.

Our imagination is engaged when we do things that are imaginative. That doesn't mean every creative idea only comes after a surf session, but it does mean that you have to put the same amount of energy into your play as you do your work, and then pay attention.

As I think about my time in San Diego, I can see that my greatest boost of imagination and resourcefulness came during this month, well over halfway into the project.

That makes me wonder — maybe one of the reasons imagination is hard to come by is because it necessitates a dose of endurance and observation. When we do something challenging for a long period of time, we're forced to search deep within ourselves and our surroundings to find new ways around those challenges.

And, there, just around the corner from your lowest point, underneath your biggest obstacle, and next to your surfboard — that's where you'll find imagination.

IMAGI-NATION DOESN'T SIT STILL.

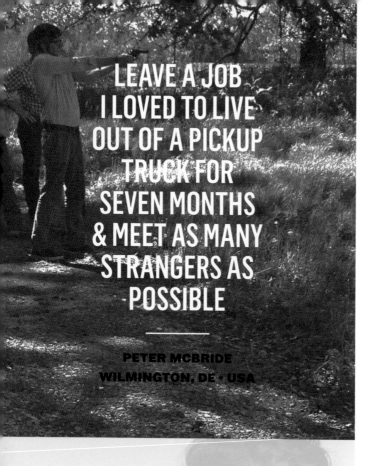

LEAVE A JOB
I LOVED TO LIVE
OUT OF A PICKUP
TRUCK FOR
SEVEN MONTHS
& MEET AS MANY
STRANGERS AS
POSSIBLE

PETER MCBRIDE
WILMINGTON, DE * USA

MAKE A
STAND-UP
COMEDY
HALF-HOUR
SPECIAL FOR
TELEVISION

BETH STELLING
LOS ANGELES, CA * USA

←

Since I was fourteen years old, I've wanted to travel the country in a Class A motorhome. A few years ago, at 25, I bought one. Four months later, I quit my job, sold the RV, and bought a pickup truck. On February 29th, 2012, I started driving around the country. My plan was simple: meet as many strangers and visit as many national parks as possible. To a curious and newly unemployed twenty-something with a soft spot for long-distance running, these sound like two of our country's most prized possessions. The adventure took me in every direction. I stopped at flea markets in Alabama and learned how to make an alligator-jaw knife in Louisiana. I spent ten days with an artist in Texas and three weeks working at an antique shop in Kansas. I got lost at 13,000 feet in Colorado, hiked up to 14,000, found the peak, and slid back down. I ran down the Grand Canyon in 85 minutes and found a new friend from Serbia at the bottom. We hiked back up together — in seven and a half hours. I took long walks with park rangers in Yosemite and had long talks with coffee-goers at McDonald's. I learned that it's not hard to meet people when you can deliver lines they've never heard before, like, "Most nights I just sleep in my truck," or, "I'm from Delaware." Lots of people had questions and everyone had a story. I listened a lot. In Seattle, I found Camp Korey, a non-profit summer camp for children with life-threatening illnesses. I volunteered for two weeks and left with a much clearer understanding of what I want to do with my life. After more than six months and 16,000 miles, I was done traveling.

The scales of generosity had tipped in my favor. Now, I'm looking for a way to give back — something at the intersection of entrepreneurship and social change. Pretty vague, I agree. So in the meantime, I'm working at a running store in Deleware and treating myself to the occasional cup of coffee (and conversation) at McDonald's.

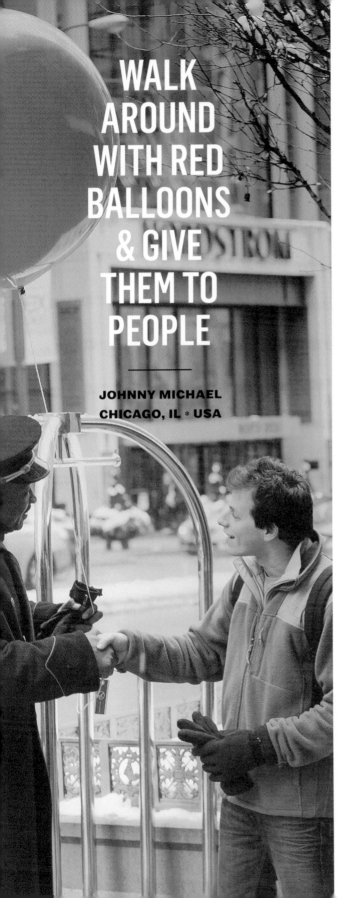

WALK AROUND WITH RED BALLOONS & GIVE THEM TO PEOPLE

JOHNNY MICHAEL
CHICAGO, IL ∗ USA

I just wanted to go out into the world and say hello. I had an ambition to meet more people, to get out there, and introduce myself.

Not to sell anything. Not to ask for anything in return. Just to make a connection and hopefully make someone's day.

I needed a simple and spontaneous solution.

So I filled up a red balloon, walked around the city, and eventually gave it to a kid. It was a good day.

Some people thought I was crazy. Some found it adorable.

A red balloon has this sort of magical charm, a radiating aura of joy. People look me in the eye. I get a lot of smirks and smiles. People say hello, they tell me, "Nice balloon you got there!" Pointing happens, lots of nudges and "Look at this guy." Some even snap photos. I'll admit it, people do laugh at me and I'm sure remarks about my intelligence aren't always positive. When I first started, my friends thought I was losing it. My sister thought I was a weirdo. My brother thought I was sexually confused. My dad was just plain confused, most likely wondering who's having a birthday. And my mom? She just thought it was cute and wanted me to stay safe.

So with all that, plus the helium shortage, I decided to order bigger balloons.

Over time people around me came to understand my heart is wrapped around my intentions. They saw the beauty of the simple gesture and how it hoists a little happiness in the air. More importantly, they saw how this teeny-tiny act could eventually create change. They saw the good and I keep seeing it too.

Walking around with red balloons most certainly will not solve the world's problems, but I do believe it's a stride in the right direction. It's a statement of my happiness and a little introduction of good things to come.

←

SEATTLE
WA
USA

CREATE A SECRET COMMUNITY IN A HIDDEN WINE CELLAR

I wanted to give a toast. That's where this all started. We were walking one night with some friends and saw this store-front space with a big table and a catered party taking place. As we looked in the window, I said, "I want to have a party like that so I can give a toast. I want to invite a bunch of people to sit at a long table and then I will stand up and give a speech, and raise a glass." We joked about the absurdity of it and kept walking. Many months later, we found ourselves in the decantering room of a wine cellar owned by a friend, tucked away in the basement of an old building in Ballard, WA. A friend mentioned that the space deserved to be used, but she didn't know what to do with it.

And then I remembered the toast.

I retold the scene of the table with the people and talked about my desire to invite people to come and hear me toast. As the conversation continued, that event turned into a series of events with a few friends, each of whom are given the opportunity to share an experience with the group. Invitations went out and a group of about 15 people was formed. And then the monthly gatherings commenced. I gave a speech at the head of a long beautiful table to people ready to listen and ask questions.

That evening, my voice mattered. And others have followed, with stories, with songs, with dreaming, with imagining, with beautiful glimpses of individuality, with moments of vulnerability, of gravity, and of levity. It has been a journey of hearing, seeing, and knowing one another.

If I've learned anything, it's that happiness exists in the strangest of places: in sleepy Sunday mornings and summer concert crowds, trail runs and Manhattan rooftops; in '50's music and watercolors, museum corridors and antiquated textbooks; in earnest 4 a.m. conversations and cups of coffee and protégées and official letters and T.S. Eliot and small kindnesses and run-on-sentences and — perhaps most strangely and importantly of all — in ourselves.

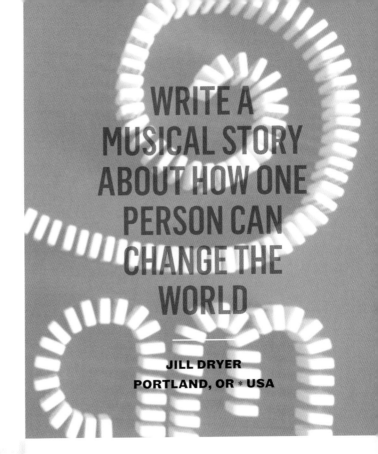

WRITE A MUSICAL STORY ABOUT HOW ONE PERSON CAN CHANGE THE WORLD

JILL DRYER
PORTLAND, OR ∗ USA

BE MORE CLEVER, COMPASSIONATE, & OPEN TO CHANGE

ELLEN MILLER
MORRIS PLAINS, NJ ∗ USA

I chose to write a story and musical score called *Dream* because I was inspired by the stories of the many people who have touched my life. People who took leaps at all ages and walks of life. Those who went against the odds, believed in something bigger, and made me feel like anything was possible.

The show is about dreamers and realists and why having a dream elevates, inspires and connects us to others. Dreams are the lifeblood of humanity. And, like our lead character, we're on an accidental journey to discover our true purpose in life.

We're learning that the best way to survive is to push for what we believe in and make choices accordingly — without fear.

GOING RIGHT

—

URBAN OFFERING
SHANGHAI, CHINA

WHEN I WAS A KID, LANGUAGE WAS A BIT OF A STRUGGLE.

——————

Surrounded by my Arabic-speaking parents at home and my English-speaking friends and teachers at school, I would often find myself in some pretty confusing, and hilarious, vocabulary mix-ups.

Take, for example, the word "right." As I simultaneously tried to learn the difference between left and right, and right and wrong, both definitions seemed to meld into one.

If someone would ask me, "Should we go right?" while driving, I would strongly answer, "Always go right! You should always go right!"

To this day when I'm stuck between going left or right, I laugh to myself, and still instinctively choose right.

By September, I had seen a wide array of businesses, projects, and teams in motion and I had gotten glimpses of ways to cut corners, cheat, or just make poor choices. Running my own project at the same time, I had begun to understand how easy it could be to start justifying the small things.

"Is it a big deal if I take this without asking?"

"They won't mind if I clock a few extra hours."

"No one will care if I show up later than I said I would."

It's humbling to admit that all of those thoughts crossed my mind at some point throughout this project, and each time, I realized I was deciding between left or right in a much bigger way than ever before.

Which way would I choose? Where would it lead?

WOVEN TOGETHER

As I continued studying social enterprise, I began to realize that these questions and decisions — left or right — extended far beyond my own personal actions. Specifically, I started learning about the challenges facing for-profit businesses who wanted to support and empower communities, while still maintaining quality, ethics, and profit. I was intrigued.

The opportunity to learn more came from my friend JP Chookaszian. He and his family had been working tirelessly to launch Urban Offering, a business focused on providing custom men's suits at an affordable cost while donating a portion of the sales to non-profits in the communities where the clothes were manufactured and distributed.

The Urban Offering team is made up of JP and Dave Chookaszian, two young, business-minded brothers, Don Chookaszian, their father and a lifetime entrepreneur, and Sharbel Shamoon, a smart and savvy sales rep. As they planned an upcoming trip in September to visit their suppliers in China, we discussed the possibility of me joining in.

After brainstorming, the team decided that my role would be one part journalist, documenting the trip through blog posts and photos, and one part business strategist. They asked me to provide a fresh perspective on their plans for positively impacting communities, and how to best engage clients, partners, and even competitors; putting nearly everything I learned from the year so far to the test.

I snagged my Chinese Visa and, after fourteen hours of travel on trains and planes, found myself in Shanghai with a team I had never even met face-to-face.

It didn't take long to realize that this trip and this team were special.

One of the first things I noticed was how their interactions differed from the other teams I had worked with. As a family business, these guys didn't just share the same ideas, they came from the same places. And even though each team member was unique, they were woven together by a solid bond, a common passion, and a bold mission. This tie would permeate everything about their story and their brand.

Second, I saw how the Urban Offering team demonstrated a genuine interest in each person they worked with. They didn't just focus on doing business, but took the time to make sure their Chinese teammates really felt valued and included; bringing gifts, sharing updates on the final products, and passing family photos from their time together back in Chicago.

Some of this is simply good business — but it is also just plain good, and from my point of view, the right way to do things.

SUITS WITH A SOUL

I spent much of my time during and after our trip to China with Dave, the team's numbers guy. He was enrolled in The Kellogg School of Business, my dream school when exploring MBA programs the year before. We shared a passion for creating businesses sparked out of a mission to meet needs and give back.

As Dave and I talked about ways to make sure Urban Offering was doing everything with the utmost attention to ethics, it was clear that there was absolutely no room for cutting corners in his mind. Taxes, shipping, employee wages, and working conditions — everything had to be examined and done well.

But the team wasn't just concerned with avoiding the wrong things, they were also dedicated to actively doing the right things; a commitment I saw for myself through their partnership with an inspiring non-profit in Asia called The Starfish Project. This

THERE WAS NO ROOM FOR CUTTING CORNERS.

123

organization empowers exploited women in Asia by providing them with counseling, housing, health services, and vocational training for alternate employment through their jewelry-making business.

We met the director, Pip Nelson, for dinner while we were in town and spent the entire time intently listening and learning about the issues. She could barely sneak in a bite as we peppered her with questions and hung on her every word.

BEING YOU

During the trip, I carried a small camera with me everywhere we went; documenting each moment through quick videos and a plethora of photos. At the end of every day, I uploaded the images and each morning I would wake up before the team and post them on a daily blog for their audience to read back home.

This unique role was tiring, but it forced me to pay attention to every detail as I took notes, recorded what I was learning, and shared insights on holes I was seeing.

My outside perspective on these details fostered much-needed conversations, and we spent hours talking about how the Urban Offering team should share their story and interact with their customers.

"Rather than trying to be cool, hip, or spectacular, just show your true colors as a family," I suggested. "Let the fact that you are family influence the rest of your relationships: your partners, your customers, and your community. That's a unique story that needs to be told — be who you are."

Oftentimes when we're starting something new, we look around and think that being excellent means being the most polished, but it doesn't.

Being excellent means being wholly you. If you constantly compare yourself to others, you'll be inclined to simply get ahead of them or try beating them on their own terms, instead of focusing on your own unique story. That fight, that race, is a consuming one — and is often when and where people begin to cut corners.

Nothing could be more dangerous.

THE ETHICS OF SOCIAL CHANGE

These days, social change is a popular topic. Online platforms are making 'doing good' easier than ever, and opportunities to support worthy causes are popping up around every corner.

While we all want to make a difference, I saw firsthand in September that this is not a simple discussion. The ethics of doing business and being socially responsible in an increasingly global world are intricate and complicated.

In our zeal to try to make the world better, it's the small every-day decisions that need our attention, because these seemingly insignificant choices have power; the power to care for others or to harm them, the power to create opportunities or to destroy them, the power to empower or to exploit.

Ignorance is no longer an excuse, and good intentions are not enough. The only way things will change for the better is if we each commit to making choices — big and small — that are full of integrity and value. We are faced with these decisions every day, decisions that will take us, little by little, in the direction we choose.

So please, do us all a favor...

Go right.

SEP 01

@victorsaad: One year ago, I received my last paycheck from my full-time job. What a wild ride this has been.

125

LAUNCH A SOCIALLY CONSCIOUS CUSTOM FASHION COMPANY

JP, DAVE, & DON CHOOKASZIAN
CHICAGO, IL ∗ USA

This was a desire to partner together as a family and focus on something that would wed several passions — to create something beautiful and do good with it.

At our low points, the stress felt like paralysis, but eventually we realized something great was coming together.

I learned quickly, you don't have to be a pure "entrepreneur" to start something. You just have to find something you have a sincere passion for and know a little something about. I guess that, and a willing sense of naivety, because it's always more work than you can ever imagine.

I know there are nearly endless opportunities for people to be generous throughout their daily activities and I wanted to help drive that. First opportunity: invite local businesses to sell coupons and give a portion of the proceeds to non-profits. The concept of daily deals wasn't new, but I thought we needed more of it in our community. Our idea was simply to create a website that helped non-profits raise money and awareness by promoting local daily deals. 90% of the proceeds would support non-profits.

I valued change and impact more than I cared how uncomfortable I felt about sales and strangers. I think that's what it takes to make big things happen — there has to be a commitment to values that supercede emotions.

START A THOUGHTFUL MAID BUSINESS

NICK LEFORS
CALIFORNIA * USA

CREATE A TOOL THAT HELPS PEOPLE BUY LOCAL & SUPPORT NON-PROFITS

AMY KAUFFMAN
ROCHESTER, NY * USA

I've always wanted to start a business, and after some research, I decided to start a maid business with an emphasis on online ordering and customer service.

Currently, one of my roommates works for Krochet Kids, a non-profit organization that empowers women in Uganda. I connected the two dots when putting together my business plan — a percentage of all sales would go to Krochet Kids and the work they're doing. Cleaning with a cause!

We're just getting started now, so we only have two cleaners; but it's been neat to be able to provide a steady source of income for people in my community. And I love the smirk that crosses people's face when I share my idea, and they get it.

NOTE: "And in case you were wondering, Nick's favorite candy bar is 100 Grand. He claims it to be prophetic. He also prefers ankle socks over tube."

JOURNEY TO JAPAN TO DEVELOP A BUSINESS & COMMUNITY THAT ORGANICALLY GROWS A SPECIALTY TEA INDUSTRY

ELYSE PETERSON
HONOLULU, HI * USA

The two things that are my motivation these days are tea and collaboration.

During my last semester of my graduate program, I had to choose between doing a final project near home or take a semester trip to Japan to learn about tea farming first hand.

I chose Japan.

Within the first few weeks, I second-guessed my decision. It was cold and uncomfortable and I knew no one. But the challenge caused me to recall why I was there in the first place. I spent time learning from the farmers and even met with others who visited from India and Indonesia. We chatted about the vision of an organization that supported farmers. The tea business is so simple, yet they knew that coming together could move mountains and make the world a better place with their craft.

I returned to Hawaii to create a tea brand and distribution system. From the start, we had opportunities to increase our margins that would require us to deviate from our social mission.

We passed on those opportunities.

Instead of sourcing lower-priced tea which could make us more attractive in the market, we created something that supports and empowers independent tea growers. Our prices may be higher but we have identified a community that is just as passionate as us about our mission to connect tea growers with tea lovers.

The most valuable lesson I have learned is that people do care. We have built a community of thousands of conscious tea lovers around the world who want to contribute to our effort to create a more transparent tea industry. If you are passionate about something, it is your responsibility to share that passion with others because action will inevitably manifest.

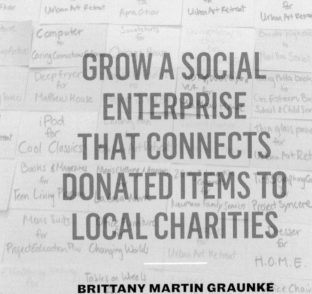

GROW A SOCIAL ENTERPRISE THAT CONNECTS DONATED ITEMS TO LOCAL CHARITIES

BRITTANY MARTIN GRAUNKE
CHICAGO, IL ＊ USA

Last year, I began to notice a massive disconnection. People and companies had things they no longer needed, while non-profits were in need of those very items; but there was no easy way for them to find each other. I wanted to fix this. I spoke to 200+ people during a 6-month period and learned more about how I could solve the problem using technology. I began wondering how I could turn this into a business and if it wasn't such a crazy idea to just quit my job and do it.

Along the way, I've learned it takes extra work to implement your personal core values into a business. But when your business is on a mission to make the world better, it becomes a little easier. Everyone on our team holds the same values and we work hard to be honest about why we're here and the way we work.

FAMILY

—————

PROJECT 7
COSTA MESA, CA

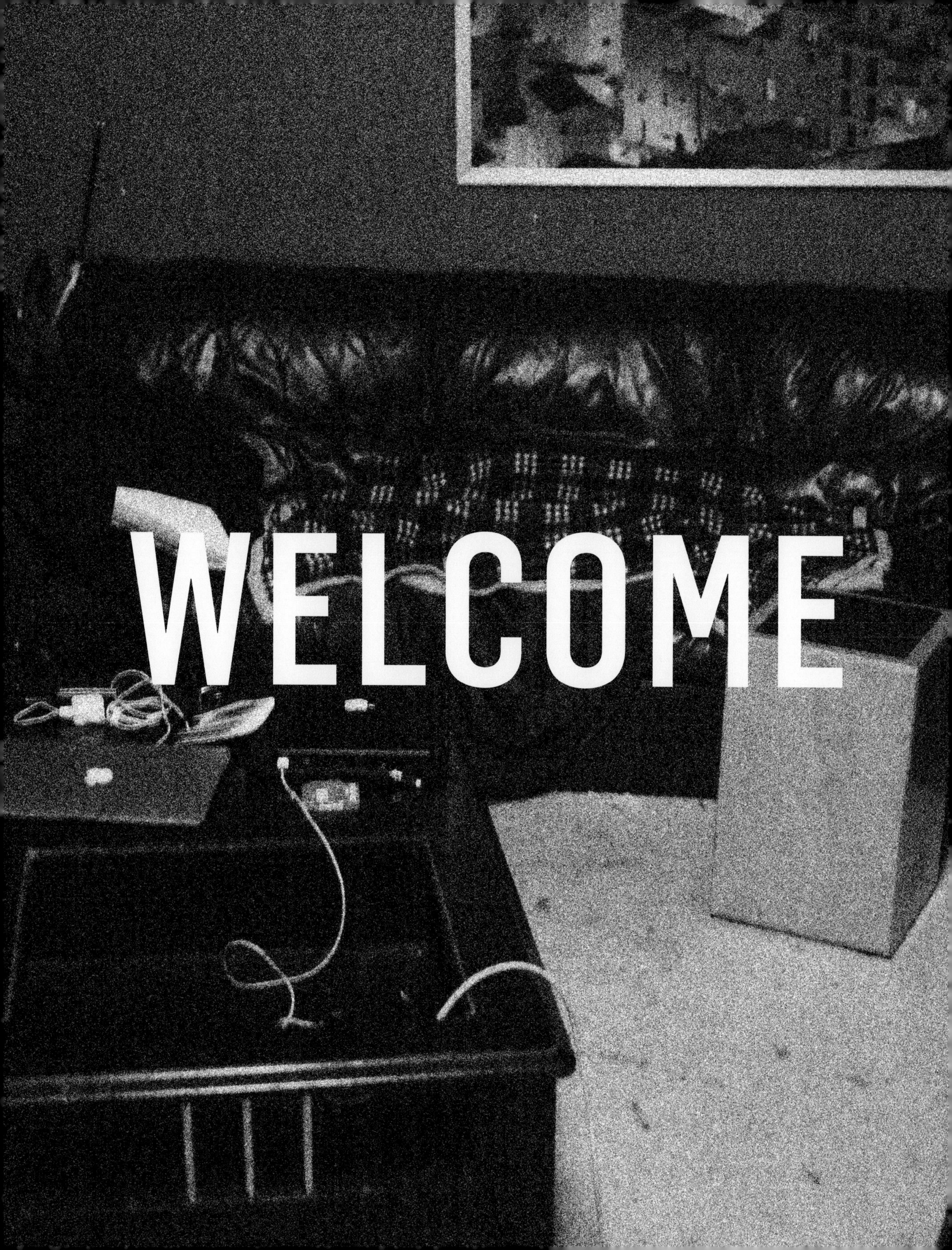
WELCOME

MY MOTHER IS THE MOST HOSPITABLE PERSON ON THE PLANET.

———————

She loves inviting people into our home, and when I was younger, we hosted everyone from students to random people we met at the mall. Possessing the astounding ability to effortlessly cook enough food to feed a small army, she's a combination of *Mary Poppins* and the mother from the film *My Big Fat Greek Wedding*.

But the most amazing thing about my mother isn't her delicious Middle Eastern cooking, it's the way she makes people feel included. When you sit at my mother's table, you're not just an outsider, a spectator, or another mouth to feed. When you sit at her table, you belong; you're family.

Throughout The Leap Year Project, I have seen the benefits of working in community. From Threadless in March to Fifty & Fifty in August, I saw the power of gathering around an idea or movement and inviting others to join.

But even as the value of community became more evident, I was also beginning to learn the significance of taking relationships to the next level, of moving one step further — from ideas to people, from community to family.

As I looked around, I found myself in the midst of something that was bigger than just me and my friends.

THE LEAP YEAR PROJECT HAD PLACED ME RIGHT IN THE MIDST OF AN EXTENDED FAMILY; A GROUP OF PEOPLE WHO WOULD SURROUND AND SUPPORT ME THROUGHOUT OCTOBER AND THE REST OF THE YEAR.

SEVEN GUYS, ONE HOUSE, AND A THRIVING ANT POPULATION

HUNTING FOR HOME

Every month away from Chicago, I found a place to call home just in the nick of time; my cousin Fady in Cairo, Amber's place in Boulder, Sam's place in Seattle, and Bryan's place in San Diego, among others.

But in October, I was headed to Costa Mesa, California, to spend time working with Project 7, and no amount of tweets, emails, Facebook statuses, or personal appeals returned any leads for a place to stay. Unexpectedly, a good friend offered to pay for two nights in a hotel room, so I took the chance and hopped the next flight to Orange County.

I had two nights to find somewhere to stay.

After an unsuccessful first day, I continued my quest — house-sitting and couch surfing — until two and a half weeks later when I finally landed at a bachelor pad called The Hamilton House.

The seven guys had shoved all of the typical garage tools, cabinets, bikes, and motorcycles to the sides of the garage, laid down a few rugs, added couches and a coffee table in the center, and hung one picture on the wall. This was my room.

Seven guys, one house, and a thriving ant population.

It was...interesting, to say the least, but for now, it was home.

FAMILY FIRST

Project 7, founded by a social entrepreneur named Tyler Merrick in 2008, is a product-based company with a mission to "change the score" for those in need around the world.

Through the production and sale of everyday items such as coffee, mints, bottled water, gum, and apparel, Project 7 supports seven specific areas: Feed the Hungry, Heal the Sick, Hope for Peace,

House the Homeless, Quench the Thirsty, Teach Them Well, and Save the Earth.

Although I had been a big fan of the company since I first saw their products at a coffee shop a few years prior, the only person I had met was Tyler.

As we began to spend more time together, I noticed how often the topic of family surfaced in our discussions. Tyler had spent years working alongside his father in a family business, and although there were obvious challenges, both men sought to keep their relationship a healthy one.

With his father and his wife as his closest confidants and advisers, it was clear how significantly the value of family shaped the way Tyler led Project 7.

More than achieving extreme success or exponential growth, Tyler wanted to build a team that created and embraced a culture of family; a team based on the ideals of intentional thought and care.

Little did I know, these values would shape more of the next two months than I expected.

TEAMING UP

Tyler was initially skeptical about how beneficial a mere 30 days at Project 7 would be, and he challenged me to try things fast and learn as much as I could.

With free rein to interview the staff and decide where I could be most helpful, I had the opportunity to work with a team of talented people on a wide variety of projects, ranging from rethinking their website to developing a new gum flavor.

Each day pushed me well outside my comfort zone and my areas of expertise; I recognized immediately that the entire team was smarter and more experienced than I was. But that was okay; we were all on the same team.

OCT 04

@victorsaad: One of this month's #lyproject lessons: Being helpful comes before being creative.

FAMILY IS IN IT FOR THE LONG-HAUL.

It was sinking in that the people who made up these teams I admired so much, were just that — people. They weren't just a company, a case study, or a chance for me to test out my newest theories.

When a group of people share the same values and mission, a committed drive to do whatever it takes, and a genuine investment in one another, something starts to shift. A bond is developed; one that can only come from learning from one another, working together, and putting others first.

And as these ties are strengthened, we not only build bridges, we begin giving of ourselves; sharing, inspiring, serving.

EXTENDED FAMILY

In addition to the increasing feeling of closeness with the Project 7 team, I also began to notice an astonishing amount of invitations — often from the most unlikely, but lovely people.

First there was Jim, the guy I met on the plane from Chicago, who was so curious about my weird life that he insisted on taking me out to dinner with a group of his friends.

Then, a couple of Leapers who heard I was in the area invited me to their home to share stories of their individual leaps and even their Leap Day Meetup.

On top of that, a crew of newfound friends from Los Angeles hosted me on several occasions, an incredible couple named Ryan and Lacey made sure to check on me almost daily, and some generous friends opened their home for a few weekend retreats.

As I looked around, I began to realize something amazing: after nearly a year of work, all of my hopes to not just do this thing alone, but to inspire and bring others along were coming to fruition.

Throughout The Leap Year Project, I constantly faced giant hurdles; things I didn't know, projects I couldn't complete. In those moments, I was often hesitant to ask for help.

But by October, I was starting to understand that when you share your hurdle with someone, it gives them an opportunity to contribute — to open their home, prepare a meal, write a note — and therefore be part of something bigger. Leaping, and asking for help along the way, reminds us that we are in this together.

Throughout the year, I witnessed people trying great things, sharing ideas and lessons, and supporting each other along the way. The project was developing from a group of individuals taking risks into an extended family of friends and teammates.

FAMILY TIME

By the end of October, I had learned that starting anything is an opportunity to build a team, a community, and that with time, those bonds grow stronger.

The Project 7 team worked hard, shared meals, laughed a lot, and dreamt big. But built on the foundation of investing in and serving one another, they intentionally grew beyond just a community of people co-laboring towards a goal, into a family creating something meaningful together.

When a community deepens its connection, something great begins to happen. Often geographically-based and built around an idea rather than a dedication to one another, communities tend to shift, adapt, and change.

Family, on the other hand, is in it for the long-haul; prioritizing people over circumstances, and the idea of together over anything else.

Every now and then, especially during a Leap, look around at who brings you in and who sticks with you.

You'll find that they'll become more than friends.

They'll become family.

OCT 17

Empathy +
imagination +
diligence lead
to surprising places.

137

EACH OF US WILL PICK A SERVICE PROJECT & THE ENTIRE FAMILY WILL DO IT TOGETHER

JUSTIN, SARAH, QUINN, AVA, JACKSON, & MACKENZIE AHRENS
GENEVA, IL * USA

MY DAUGHTERS & I WILL DO 12 DIFFERENT PROJECTS THAT BENEFIT OTHERS IN NEED, THE ENVIRONMENT, OR ANIMALS

ANN, SOPHIA, & OLIVIA
RINKENBERGER
SCANDIA, MN * USA

2012 began in a rather challenging way: my father died on January 5th after a multi-year battle with Alzheimer's Disease.

Many of the projects stemmed from his values that he passed onto me, and, in turn, I have passed onto my daughters. We have learned that each person can make a difference in the world...even if s/he is struggling — financially, emotionally, or physically. There's always something that can be done to help.

The projects taught us to work together — especially when it came to finding items to donate each month. We cleaned closets, drawers, bookshelves, and entire rooms of our home. The work was difficult, but we remembered what we were working towards and kept the bigger picture in mind.

GET OUR FOSTER CARE LICENSE BY THE END OF 2012 AND START PROVIDING A SAFE & LOVING PLACE FOR CHILDREN WHO NEED IT

LIZ & ANDY YOUNG
CHICAGO, IL * USA

I have four amazing kids and a wife that loves me (for some weird reason). Wanting to make an impact in the world as a family, we decided to do something together.

So, each family member was assigned two months out of the year where they would choose a project all of us could complete together.

The questions we had as parents were: "Will it matter to them? Will they see differently? Will they care? Will they see parts of the world they didn't before, and most importantly, will they see that they can make a difference?"

The most challenging part of the year was when we detoured our vacation to visit a Hurricane Katrina victim to help her landscape her home. The neighborhood was different than ours; the kids were unsure and hesitant. That day we battled crazy vines, fire ants, being in a new place, heat and humidity, emotions — the kids felt overwhelmed. They wanted to go back to the beach. But then something awesome happened: accomplishment. By the end of the day, we helped Mrs. B. feel a little more at home, and all of us knew it was worth it.

Later in the year, we worked with the organization Feed My Starving Children. During cleanup time we simply did what we needed to do, no complaints. At the end of the day, we got to taste the food and learned it was going to Haiti. We looked at the map and saw the place that the kids had only heard of; we all smiled at each other. The leader explained we filled 79 boxes, which totaled 17,064 meals. We were told we were part of feeding 47 people for an entire year. The kids said, "Mom and Dad, that is super cool. We did that! We should totally do this again." And you know what, they were right. It was super cool.

Maybe, just maybe, we are making a dent.

For quite a while, my husband and I have felt compelled to become foster parents and show love and support to children who have experienced loss, trauma, and many other heartaches. This year, we decided to turn our lives upside down and get our foster care license. We hope to invite sibling groups of older kids (ages 4-9) into our home. Over 70% of kids in the foster care system come into the system with a sibling. If no home is found that can take the group, the kids are split up and taken away from what might be the only stable relationship they've ever known. Our house is small, but we want to open it up for children and do our part to keep sibling groups together.

It has been challenging and heart-wrenching to learn about the situations children in foster care come from. But we believe change can happen. Now that we're licensed as foster parents, we hope to play a small part in the healing of the families in the system.

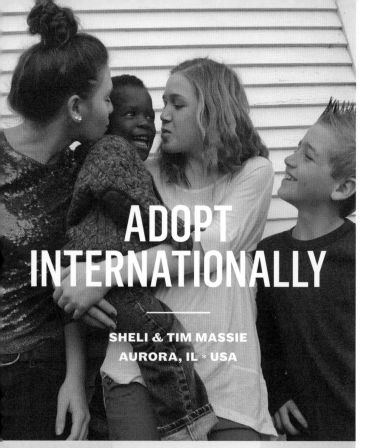

ADOPT INTERNATIONALLY

SHELI & TIM MASSIE
AURORA, IL * USA

We did not plan to adopt. It wasn't even on our radar. In 2010, we were swimming in debt raising four kids and just trying to make it paycheck to paycheck.

But all that would change with a leap and a letter from a woman at our church.

This woman had been on a trip with my wife to Sierra Leone to help in orphanages and villages in the recovering war torn areas. She herself wanted to adopt, but her family was not in a position to do so. She recognized our loving family with 4 children and said she while she could not adopt, she would put aside $10,000 towards our international adoption. The puzzle was finally beginning to make sense. From there, garage sales, fund raisers, friends, family, etc. helped us raise the rest of what we needed.

And now Ephraim Kwagala is a part of our family.

←

FIND MY BIOLOGICAL FATHER

NICK GAINES
CHICAGO, IL * USA

I've spent my entire adult life wondering if God would allow me to meet my dad. I wondered what it would be like to see him. Would there be tears? Laughter? Anger? Or would I realize I wasn't ready and just walk away?

After some research, and weeks of phone calls and emails, we finally met.

We spent the entire day together. I still can't get over our similarities: taste in food, how we talk and walk, our flatfootedness. I could go on and on.

I even met the rest of the family — nearly all of them tall and athletic. In fact, I am the "small one" in the family.

All of it went better than imagined.

I will never forget this day.

DETROIT
MI
USA

⌄

My wife and I had been wanting to move somewhere where we had more of an impact and stake in the future.

Six months into living here I am now a photographer covering Detroit and it's revitalization. We are loving the city and the change in lifestyle.

There certainly are challenges, practical things like grocery stores, crime, transportation. Detroit is quite different than Boulder. One of the hardest things is having young children in a city with a lack of parks, educational opportunities and simple things like high chairs in restaurants. But we want to partner with those that have come before us and have been championing this city for decades. We want to love people, be good neighbors, and show that Detroit is a place where family can thrive.

MOVE FROM
BOULDER→DETROIT

For years I tried getting my father's attention with my success, awards, recognition — to no avail. This year, I simply tried to connect with my father. I committed to writing him a letter each month of the year.

I found it quite difficult at first, to even know what to write him. But as I continued to write, I found that it became easier. Letters to my father allowed me to share openly with him my musings on life, my understanding of the world, my questions while becoming a man, my desire to know him more deeply, and my desire to see him grow and challenge himself.

I have seen tremendous growth in my own comfort and ability to share with him, and have even begun to see him open up to me. It has been refreshing.

As I have shared my story with others I have been surprised to hear how many men (and women) have strained relationships with their own fathers. I'd like to think that my story has given hope and encouragement to do the same.

There is something about committing thoughts and feelings to paper in ink — something that makes it a bit more honest and raw than re-typing a line in an email. It often allows me to communicate things with my father that I may otherwise hold back, or not completely finish in a conversation. And, I know that he has been saving some of my letters, something far more valuable than a folder in an inbox.

$\longrightarrow$

TRAVEL OVER 5,700 MILES TO SUPPORT FOSTER KIDS

WRITE LETTERS TO MY FATHER

NILES EMERICK
DENVER, CO ∗ USA

TRENTON
NJ
USA

Becoming a foster parent in 2006 changed my life. I cared for children in my home that had been through trauma and challenges that I couldn't imagine. So, I created a non-profit (One Simple Wish) to empower people in the community to support children in foster care. In May 2012, I decided to take a 30-day trip in an RV for National Foster Care Awareness Month to bring to light the stories of these children who were being served by different communities.

Along the way, I met Charles. He was 15 with special needs and legally free for adoption, which means that his parents' rights had been terminated. His wish was just to play outside with friends and to get some Legos. It was so simple. So, we came there with Legos and my children and played all afternoon. He hugged them so many times. He smiled constantly. You could tell that all he wanted was someone to love him.

What I learned most of all from my 5,700 mile journey is that above all else, family is what matters most — however you define that. Family doesn't have to be a mom, dad, and kids. It can be any crazy, interesting mix of people who love and support each other unconditionally. There is no love like the love of a family; there for your terrible times and there for your awesome times. The children we met who came out of this broken child welfare system whole and happy all had one thing in common — they had a village of people around them that loved them, supported them and most of all believed in them against all odds.

←

BEING PRESENT

———

**PROJECT 7
COSTA MESA, CA**

+

**UNION RESCUE
MISSION
LOS ANGELES, CA**

NICE HELMET

TOUCHDOWN

SOME LESSONS ARE LEARNED BY ACCIDENT.

———————

Though I recognized early in January that my leap was about learning and getting my hands dirty, I will admit that towards the end of the year, my fascination with superheroes had me once again dreaming of the spectacular; this time in the form of the NFL.

Like most kids, I had often fantasized about becoming a professional athlete. My athletic ability was never quite up to par, but in November, I saw the potential for my unsatisfied childhood dream to be somewhat fulfilled.

It all began in September when I found myself engaged in conversations with a friend who believed I should spend a month working alongside a professional athlete. He was convinced that my alternative educational path would be a refreshing option for someone to consider after their athletic career; a way for them to transition into jobs or learning experiences off the court or the field, while exploring how to best use their influence and resources to give back to the community.

He was especially close to one particular NFL player and we agreed that November would be spent living with him and helping him develop a plan for next steps after his career came to a close.

This idea was different than anything I had done thus far and I was intrigued. But as October was winding down, the player's situation abruptly changed and the opportunity vanished without warning.

I was disappointed, to say the least. I wanted to end well and the idea of working with a professional athlete had sparked visions of doing something both completely different and really helpful. It had the feeling of a grand finale.

Since December would be focused on compiling and writing the book, I had one week to find a way to finish the year with one final, incredible learning experience.

147

STICKING AROUND

As I went back and forth in my mind on what I should do next, Tyler and the team at Project 7 began discussing the possibility of having me stay longer. As much as I was enjoying my time there, I thought I needed to continue my commitment to complete twelve experiences in twelve months, so I declined.

Unsatisfied with my answer, Tyler continued working on me, and eventually — I agreed.

Since I had decided to stay, I was faced with another decision: should I find a new place to stay for a month, or continue to live in the garage at The Hamilton House?

By now, even though I wasn't thrilled about the living situation, I was getting to know the crew and excited to be part of their small family. So, true to the rest of November, I stayed.

This group of seven guys was bright, passionate, caring, and loyal. It may have not been most convenient, but I believed that staying could be really meaningful.

I was right.

The extra time in Costa Mesa allowed me, for the first time since embarking on The Leap Year Project, to develop deeper connections — both with the guys in the house and with acquaintances from surrounding communities.

Over the next several weeks I was able to be fully present; to stop, listen, help, and even be helped. As it turns out, these were some of the best moments of the entire year.

CATALYST → BUILDER

Many times throughout this educational journey, people have questioned whether spending a mere 30 days with an organization was beneficial. Extending my time in Costa Mesa was a chance to explore the benefits of a longer stay, moving from sparking ideas to developing them.

At the same time, I still wanted to establish one more experience to make an even twelve for the year. With Thanksgiving fast approaching, I wondered if I could use the holiday week as a unique opportunity to step out and serve somewhere in the Los Angeles community.

A good friend introduced me to Andy Bales, the CEO of Union Rescue Mission. Located in downtown Los Angeles, it serves the Skid Row district, a seemingly hopeless place where over 5,000 individuals sleep on the streets each night.

As the largest homeless shelter in the country, Union Rescue Mission seeks to care for physical, spiritual, and emotional needs, and I was excited to explore with Andy how I could be helpful.

We decided that I would join the kitchen staff during the days surrounding Thanksgiving. Between the influx of people needing a meal and volunteers wanting to help, there would be plenty of work to be done.

Although I wasn't sure what exactly I would learn through this experience, I decided to just focus on being present. Doing so would center me, once again, on what mattered most about this season of learning.

JUST SMILE

———

It's hard not to be slightly scared driving through the streets of Skid Row, but I hated myself for having those fearful thoughts. I wanted to see everyone as equals, but stories of extreme situations and the cautionary advice from friends continued to ring in my ears.

I HATED MYSELF FOR HAVING THOSE FEARFUL THOUGHTS

I parked the car in a garage below Union Rescue Mission and continued battling my fears.

"Why am I scared?"

"Why can't I see the best in people?"

"What do I think will go wrong?"

I finally walked into the basement elevators and saw the posters advertising upcoming programs — full of smiling faces.

And I thought to myself, "There it is. Just smile, Vic. Everything changes when you smile."

As I walked off the elevator, the first person I saw was a security guard directing the volunteer traffic. I mustered the biggest smile I could, signed a waiver, and found my way to the kitchen.

When I walked in, the kitchen was full of flurried activity, overflowing with recent holiday deliveries and mountains of food. Delilah, the laid-back supervisor with a dry sense of humor, showed me where I could find a hair net, an apron, and some serving gloves. I could tell she was tired and slightly overwhelmed by the amount of people who were asking questions, so I cracked a quick joke to make her smile and started helping where I could.

The next three days were a complete blur. The work was far from easy, and I found myself being continually pushed outside of my comfort zone.

At one point, one of the guys taught me how to prepare a raw turkey — something I had to do at least 100 times. I'll save you the details, but…let's just say it stretched me more than any job I've done this year. We set up our turkey frying station with fifteen fryers right on Skid Row. It was quite the sight.

With each conversation shared and plate that was filled, I found myself feeling more at ease; smiling as I began to forget about the challenges and my concerns and focusing instead on the people and their stories.

GIVING AND RECEIVING

I was planning on moving back to Chicago, living with an NFL player, and completing a grand finale experience before finishing my year. But it was only because that plan fell through that I was even thinking about staying.

It was an accident, but being present for a second month with Project 7, at the house (garage) that became more of a home, and for a few days serving on Skid Row made November one of my most memorable months of the year.

Whether you're apprenticing for a well-known leader or plunging elbow-deep into 100 turkeys, work hard and be fully present. It may not always be glamorous, but there is value in sticking around and asking that small, but powerful question, "How can I help?"

Each day, we decide where to focus our attention. We are often drawn to whatever is new and spectacular — sometimes it's out of a desire to pursue the latest and greatest, while other times it's the simple wish to be a little more comfortable.

In these moments we need to be careful, because rushing off too quickly may mean missing the most valuable lessons.

I loved moving to new places, but this month I needed to stay, build deeper relationships, and serve those around me.

In doing so, I received much more than I ever could have given.

Lesson learned.

eleven down ... One to go!

COLOMBO
SRI LANKA

I am the sole creator of each workshop, composing a medley of theatre games, arts, crafts, and creative writing. It takes me completely out of my comfort zone. I travel unchaperoned by train each week to these villages and conduct my workshops among children who only speak Tamil, of which I know just a handful of phrases.

We are rehearsing for a play at the moment and I feel a sense of joy in the way they have grown over the past year. I wanted to create a safe space for the children to be comfortable and to be themselves, and seeing them rehearse, I believe that space now exists. The children still regard me as a teacher, yet joke and play with me in a way that makes it clear that they are completely at ease.

It's been an incredibly rewarding year.

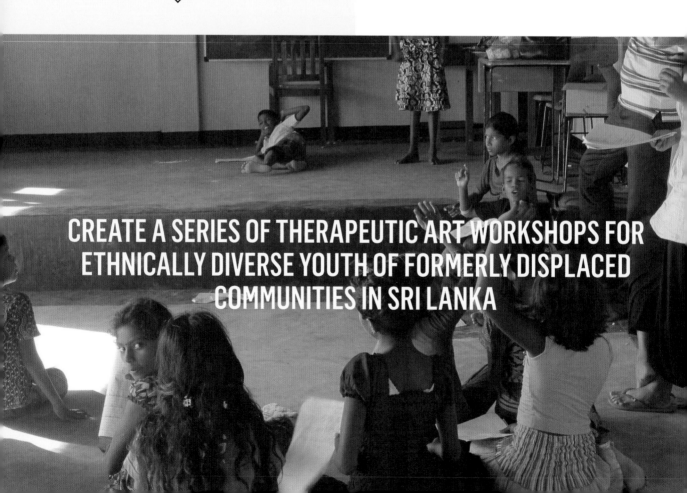

CREATE A SERIES OF THERAPEUTIC ART WORKSHOPS FOR ETHNICALLY DIVERSE YOUTH OF FORMERLY DISPLACED COMMUNITIES IN SRI LANKA

MOVE TO RURAL INDIA TO PILOT A FAMILY PLANNING PROGRAM AMONG MARGINALIZED WOMEN IN TRIBAL COMMUNITIES

SARAH KAMMERER
CHICAGO, IL * USA

At the age of 27, I returned to get my Master's in Public Health. Three months after graduating in May 2012, I took my leap: I departed for my third and longest trip to India on a Fullbright Research Grant. I spent 9 months developing, implementing and evaluating a pilot program designed to address family planning issues among marginalized tribal women in a rural part of eastern India.

When I asked if I could do a small focus group of five women to get some feedback about the pilot so far, a remarkable thing happened — 33 women stayed to give their thoughts. They all spoke about how they now understood the importance of small families and educating their girls. When one woman seemed confused, the women all talked to her and said things along the lines of "But our girls have the same brains as boys and if we educate them correctly, they can do the same thing!" Afterwards, the women told us how they were spreading the word to their friends and family members about what they have learned.

It was incredible — so inspiring. I always hoped my pilot would work, but I didn't realize what that actually meant: that if it was successful, actual change would be made in these communities.

The people that I have met during this journey are not just my friends, they have become family. They welcomed a foreigner into their homes and allowed me to be a part of their work and their dreams and, along the way, they've helped me figure out my own. I've learned that things like electricity, hot water and air conditioning are things that I can actually live without. More importantly, I've learned that nothing rivals the people in your life and the experiences you share.

MOVE TO AFGHANISTAN TO
HELP TRAIN JOURNALISTS
IN CUTTING EDGE
MEDIA TECHNIQUES
GIVING DEMOCRACY A
CHANCE TO FLOURISH
————————

MEGHAN LAZIER
CHICAGO, IL * USA

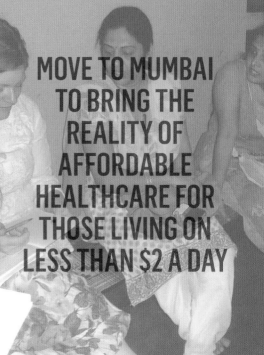

MOVE TO MUMBAI
TO BRING THE
REALITY OF
AFFORDABLE
HEALTHCARE FOR
THOSE LIVING ON
LESS THAN $2 A DAY

MUMBAI
MH
INDIA

After receiving a fellowship with LGT Venture Philanthropy, I decided to invest into what I care about most: helping others access healthcare.

The most rewarding thing is seeing the opportunity you have when you give someone hope in his/her life. Hope is an amazing little thing — whether that comes through improving your health, getting a new job, learning something new about yourself, or seeing a chronic illness in a new light.

There is no guidebook on "How to Change the World in an International Setting". You constantly have to surround yourself with people that see the small amount of traction and understand that this work takes years. India has been challenging in a myriad of ways but it was the most fulfilling experience of my life.

BALLYBOUGHAL
IRELAND

∨

RETURN TO VOLUNTEERING

I was killing time on the net and happened upon The Leap Year Project. The energy and enthusiasm emitting from the website was like sunshine. I was hooked and decided to return to volunteerism following a 6-year break.

I decided to make Mondays my volunteer day and started training as an adult literacy tutor, an issue close to my heart as one of our kids has dyslexia. This training, in turn, led me to tutor seniors in the use of IT. What a wonderful group of people they are! During our time together, family ties are strengthened, journeys are planned for holidays, fashions are researched, hotels are booked, recipes are uploaded, family trees are checked out — it's a real hive of activity for these busy people. Our youngest learner is in her mid-sixties and the oldest is mid-nineties. Their zest and enthusiasm for life is catching.

←

COLLECT SHOES FOR A COMMUNITY IN NEED

CHICAGO
IL
USA

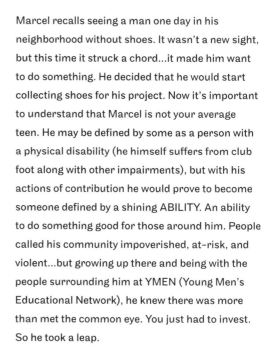

Marcel recalls seeing a man one day in his neighborhood without shoes. It wasn't a new sight, but this time it struck a chord...it made him want to do something. He decided that he would start collecting shoes for his project. Now it's important to understand that Marcel is not your average teen. He may be defined by some as a person with a physical disability (he himself suffers from club foot along with other impairments), but with his actions of contribution he would prove to become someone defined by a shining ABILITY. An ability to do something good for those around him. People called his community impoverished, at-risk, and violent...but growing up there and being with the people surrounding him at YMEN (Young Men's Educational Network), he knew there was more than met the common eye. You just had to invest. So he took a leap.

Marcel started with a pair of his own shoes. He then rallied the people around him, spending his time writing letters and sending text messages to everyone he knew. Sure enough, the community started coming together to support Marcel and his project.

Marcel set out to collect 100 shoes. After some time, he decided that 100 was not ambitious enough. He upped the ante to 300! The result? He ended up with 300 pairs. Think about it, that's 600 happy feet!

Not only did Marcel exceed expectations for his project, but he was able to show his community the determination and heart he has towards life. This project ended with a great surprise. The directors at YMEN where he was a student-mentee asked him to consider joining their staff. He gladly accepted, and now encourages others to step outside of the box and think about how they can help others.

Keep being great, Marcel.

PARTNER WITH A COMMUNITY IN KENYA TO EXPAND BUSINESS MARKETS FOR FAMILIES

———

LINDSAY VON QUALEN & DEB LUKAZEWSKI
LAKEWOOD, CA & BATAVIA, IL * USA

One of the already established trades of several people in Kibera is jewelry making. With the hope that we could help create more business for the community, we teamed up as a family to develop photo books to catalog the jewelry.

Since then, we have sold jewelry by participating in art fairs and different community events. All of the profits are being directed back to the artists. We also took the jewelry to homes, schools, and churches to give presentations and offer an opportunity to get involved.

We saw an injustice and we figured even the smallest change could offer hope for those who desperately needed it. And, to be honest, we needed to see change in order to restore a sense of hopefulness in our own hearts.

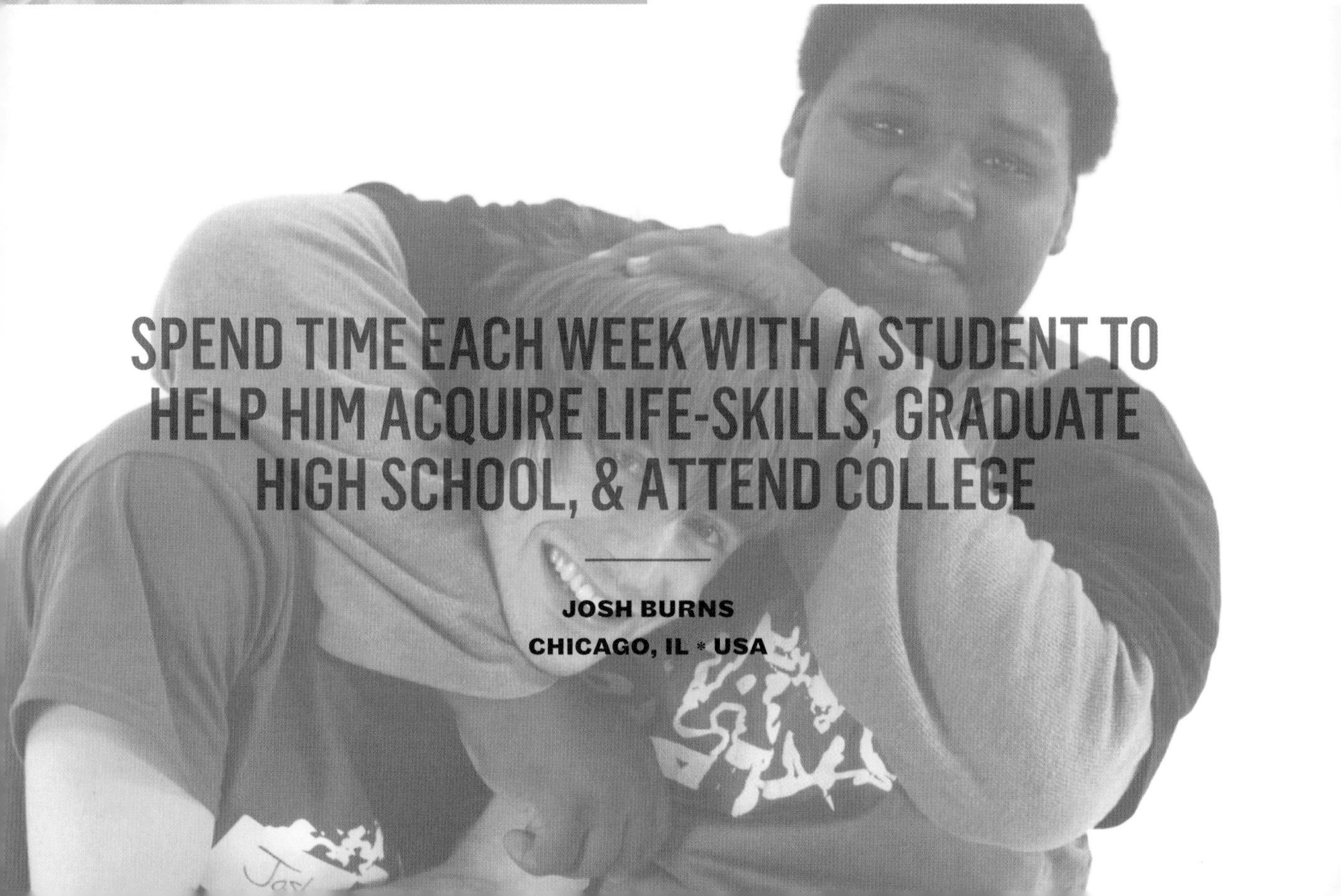

←

SPEND TIME EACH WEEK WITH A STUDENT TO HELP HIM ACQUIRE LIFE-SKILLS, GRADUATE HIGH SCHOOL, & ATTEND COLLEGE

———

JOSH BURNS
CHICAGO, IL * USA

CREATING
SOMETHING OF
VALUE

———

BOOK PROJECT
CHICAGO, IL

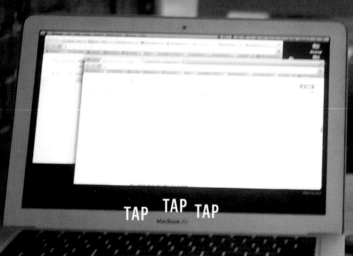

AM I CREATING SOMETHING OF VALUE?

THROUGHOUT THE YEAR, AND EVEN NOW, THAT QUESTION HAS BOTH EXCITED AND HAUNTED ME.

As The Leap Year Project came to an end, it was time for my twelfth and final project — compiling this book. A creative dissertation for my self-made MBA, the book would be a way to document what I had learned, to compile the amazing lessons and inspiration Leapers had shared, and to encourage others to continue leaping even as the calendar year changed.

Kelly Kaminski, a dear friend and volunteer Art Director for The Leap Year Project, and I had been talking about this book from the very beginning. So at the end of each month, I set aside time to write about what I had experienced and learned.

During December, a small team was ready to help organize, design, and edit those thoughts. And, thanks to the generous community surrounding the project, we were able to fund it through an online crowdfunding platform called Kickstarter. We had the research. We had the resources.

NOW ALL WE HAD TO DO WAS WRITE THE BOOK...

As I stared at a blank screen, a slew of questions raced through my mind. Was I competent and creative enough to manage a team, capture the Leaper's stories, and tell of my experiences in these few pages? The year had taught me a lot about helping people, but could I really create something valuable?

Even as I write this, I have my doubts — creating something of value is no small feat. Those things go beyond just beauty or creativity — they meet a need, one that has been seen and felt firsthand.

The question still rings in my ears: "Am I creating something of value?"

WHY LEAP?

At the very beginning of this adventure, I remember trying to explain what I was hoping to accomplish to my parents. They had already made concessions by letting me pursue an education and line of work focused on middle school and high school students.

They probably would have been on board with me quitting my job to get an MBA, but creating my own education was a different story.

The beginning of this project brought challenging conversations between my father and I, but in time he came around. Eighteen months later, when my family drove to Chicago to see me speak at a local conference, my father was beaming — introducing himself to everyone as "Za father of za Leap Year guy." It was slightly embarrassing, but it was too lovely to stop him.

Leaping changes things; not just in our own lives, but in the lives of those around us.

Too few of us are willing to move out of our comfort zones in order to explore new possibilities to create or improve something. Many of us doubt our ability to contribute, believing we are too old, too young, too poor, too inexperienced, or too busy.

Nothing could be further from the truth.

We must dream, hope, and leap. We cannot allow ourselves to become so accustomed to the problems around us that we stop being interested in their solutions. Because with each risk you take, you will inspire those around you. And for every person who sees or hears your story, as small as you think it may be, you leave behind something valuable — a glimpse, a hope, a spark.

If you don't believe me, just ask my dad.

LOOKING BACK. LEAPING FORWARD.

The entire reason I decided to pursue a year of experiential education was to learn how I could help create something significant. Whether it's a business, product, or service — I want to make things that outgrow and outlast me.

By December, I had learned a number of ways to do that, but I had also learned so much more:

I've learned that comfort is overrated, and even sometimes dangerous.

I came to know generosity far better than I know big brands, and to recognize the value of a handwritten note, a heartfelt email, an honest apology, an unexpected call, a free meal, and an open invitation.

I'm now positive that no type of work is beneath me, no name should intimidate me, and that spinach is infinitely better than Ramen. I've learned how to get a good night's sleep on any couch, manage a budget, build a team, wrestle a surfboard, and give until it hurts.

I've seen my worst and I've seen my best, and I'm ok with both of them because I know that change takes time. I've seen bad things happen, but learned that those things should fuel my resolve to do what's right, not diminish it.

I've learned that people don't want to be sold on something, they want to be invited into it; that competition is not nearly as powerful as collaboration.

I now know that success is just a word — one that is often misused and overrated. I've become a bit jaded with big ideas of changing the world, but I'm more hopeful than ever that I can help make it better.

COMPETITION IS NOT NEARLY AS POWERFUL AS COLLABORATION

I've learned that life's most difficult situations don't always need answers, they need questions, and that people have a lot to say if we take the time to listen.

But, if this year has taught me anything, it's that the most meaningful lessons are learned when our greatest fears are surpassed by our deepest convictions. It's in those challenging moments, filled with hope, uncertainty, and cautious optimism, that we find real value.

EVERYDAY HEROES

Challenging our ideas of higher education, inviting others to take their own leaps, and watching this community grow has made The Leap Year Project not only the most transformational experience of my life, but also the most valuable.

Because leaping is creating something of value. It's not about what we accomplish or acquire, it's about who we become in the process. Our responsibility is not necessarily to change the world, but to give what is ours to give; to take the risk of offering our unique contribution, to give of ourselves.

I may still start that cape company, but now I know I don't need one to do something valuable.

Leaping isn't just for the young ones among us, or the rich, the well-connected, the saints, or the heroes. It's for everyone — it's for you and me.

IT'S ABOUT WHO WE BECOME IN THE PROCESS

FIND
REAL
VALUE

DEC 20

@victorsaad: One of life's most defining moments is when we fear doing something too small more than we fear doing something too grand.

DEC 28

It's not that I think that life should always be an adventure... I just have nowhere to store my cape

The day I first began dreaming of the Change of Pace 5K sticks out very clearly in my mind. It was near the end of 2011; the air was crisp, the leaves were golden, and The Leap Year Project was rapidly approaching. As I eagerly sought inspiration for my leap, I was filled with a desire to do something meaningful; to somehow help those experiencing homelessness while inspiring others to take action with me.

But at 25 years old and with little disposable income, I was overcome with a feeling of hopelessness — what significant contribution could I possibly make? I realized that while I might not be able to single-handedly end homelessness, I had to start somewhere. And that's where this life-changing journey begins.

I had more questions than answers. All I knew was that I loved to run, and that I wanted to make a difference; to, in some small way, make life better for those experiencing homelessness — to restore dignity and inspire hope.

It wasn't long into the planning process before I reluctantly admitted that, despite my boundless enthusiasm and motivation, I could not organize the race on my own. Each time I invited someone to join with me, the Change of Pace 5K was taken to a new level. As each person offered their unique gifts and passions, contributing in a way that only they could, this once nebulous dream began to slowly take shape.

At the beginning, I thought asking others for help would diminish my leap, make it feel less significant. But as I reflect on the Change of Pace 5K and the months leading up to that memorable day, I realize that maybe planning the race wasn't the only leap I took in 2012. Maybe the bigger leap was learning to include those around me, to humble myself and trust others, to lead by equipping, empowering, and supporting. I see now that the community surrounding the race is what made it meaningful.

PLAN A 5K RACE TO RAISE FUNDS FOR & AWARENESS ABOUT HOMELESSNESS

MICHELLE LINCOLN
ST. CHARLES, IL * USA

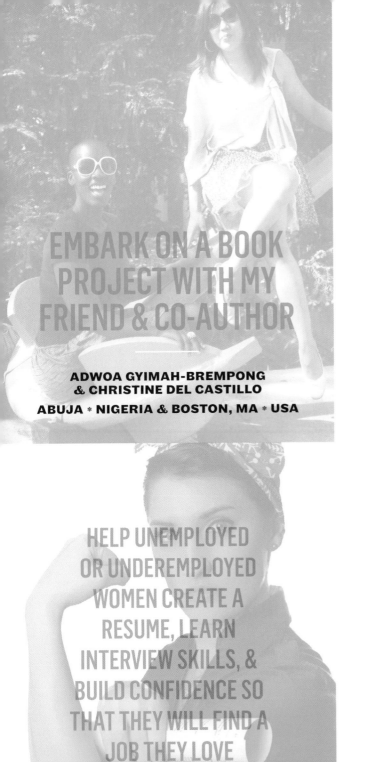

EMBARK ON A BOOK PROJECT WITH MY FRIEND & CO-AUTHOR

ADWOA GYIMAH-BREMPONG
& CHRISTINE DEL CASTILLO
ABUJA * NIGERIA & BOSTON, MA * USA

HELP UNEMPLOYED OR UNDEREMPLOYED WOMEN CREATE A RESUME, LEARN INTERVIEW SKILLS, & BUILD CONFIDENCE SO THAT THEY WILL FIND A JOB THEY LOVE

ELAINE GREEN
WOODRIDGE, IL * USA

We (Clementine and Leonessa) started writing together on the Cobblestone Contingent in 2010. It was born as a series of musings about life and love as delicate immigrant flowers in stony soils: a Filipina in Boston and the American daughter of West African immigrants in Genoa, Italy. After a year and a half of working together, The Leap Year Project offered an irresistible opportunity to dive deep, inspire each other, and take our casual writing to the next level. We committed to co-writing a book using the personal essay as our medium, and brainstormed a set of themes, a writing process, and a timeline. We would mail an essay in the form of a letter to each other once a month.

This involved meeting monthly deadlines amidst varied time zones, spotty internet connections, and busy lives. We grew as writers, experimented with collaboration, and began writing together for an external publication. Along the way, we began to see that effectively writing about personal growth would involve taking more risks in real life. Over the course of the year, one of us made the move to a more supportive continent and the other has found stable and sometimes surprising love. Now that we have racked up a few more successes and failures, we have the material we need to complete our leap. The essays are still being written, slowly — and we've learned that maybe the trick to a well-lived life is to never stop leaping at all.

NOTE: Just before this book went to print, Adwoa was informed that a proposal she designed based on her leap landed her a full tuition scholarship to a MFA program in creative writing.

PROVIDE RESTORED BICYCLES TO LOCAL SHELTERS OR INDIVIDUALS IN NEED OF INDEPENDENT TRANSPORTATION

We had the simple idea to create a stellar product, in this case great t-shirts, and then give the profits from selling said stellar product to a local cause or organization. Then we realized that in order to have the best designed t-shirts, we would need to invest in our local art and design communities. We needed to find tangible ways to support and promote artists. By doing so, they could use their art to connect with non-profits and care for the larger community. It is a beautiful vision, but also a big one.

Pursuing this dream came with many lessons, challenges, and joys. The scope of the project and our inexperience required far more planning and investigating than any of us had initially thought; but it gave us an education on the level of work that all creative ventures must face.

→

CHICAGO IL USA

HOUSTON
TX
USA

HELP STUDENTS
TRAVEL THE WORLD

JENNIFER THOMAS
CHICAGO, IL * USA

BRING AWARENESS AND
FINANCIAL SUPPORT
TO IMPORTANT LOCAL
CAUSES BY SELLING RAD
T-SHIRTS DESIGNED BY
LOCAL ARTISTS

You can have the most extraordinary teachers and the best written books, but you can only learn so much from the classroom. Meeting new people, learning languages, being surrounded by other cultures — the impact is life changing.

This year, with that idea in mind, I set out to create a system that would help students travel and learn.

My focus is on future travelers who are seeking educational and meaningful travel primarily found through program providers — academic institutions and organizations that provide volunteer, study, and teaching.

For us, this isn't about asking for money. It's about sharing the journey.

Whether you're launching a business, creating an art piece, pursuing an education, spending more time with family, serving those in need, getting healthy, or simply doing the right thing — a Leap will cost you. And it should.

A Leap will bring you face-to-face with the most difficult things you've ever attempted. And, when you're there, take note — because that is where transformation happens.

In this book, you have read stories about the risks we have taken to create change. Big or small, each was significant. We pursued hope despite the cost, knowing that a Leap's value is not found in the end result, but in the lessons we learn and the people we become.

We lept. Now, it's your turn.

WHAT RISK WOULD YOU TAKE TO CHANGE YOUR LIFE, YOUR COMMUNITY, OR YOUR WORLD FOR THE BETTER?

1 CHOOSE YOUR LEAP.
As you look at your world, what makes you sad or frustrated?
What's one risk you could take this week, month, or year to create change?

2 INVITE YOUR FRIENDS.
Who can you work with to make this happen?

3 SET SOME GOALS.
What's the first step you can take and what's a realistic deadline for your project?

4 SHARE YOUR STORY.
How will you document your experience and tell your story?

Share your Leap with us! Email: stories@leapyearproject.org or share it online with #lyproject

WHAT
LEAP
WILL
YOU
TAKE?

This book is only possible because of the 300+ people who generously contributed to The Leap Year Project Book Kickstarter Campaign.
It is **because of you** that we are able to share our stories; a collection that will inspire future Leapers for years to come.

THANK YOU.

AARON J. Amendola AARON LaMonica-Weier AJ Leon ALEX Ainslie ALEX Catedral ALEXANDRA Nelson ALICE Kaerast
ALLEN Penn AMANDA Rose AMBER Rae AMY Guterman AMY Kauffman AMY Weishuhn ANDREA Huntzicker
ANDREW R McHugh ANDREW Unger ANDY Chet ANDY Dykhouse ANDY Petek ANDY Voelker ANNA Strozik ANNE Curtis
ANTHONY Pantaleo ANTHONY Thomas ASHLEIGH Yoder ASHLEY Flitter ASHLEY Lewis ATILA Lotfi AUGUSTIN Steiner
BECCI Bartley BELINDA Leadbeatter BEN Millstein BEN Porter BEN Rugg BENJAMIN Shorofsky BETH Stelling BETHANY Doty
BLESSING Mpofu BO Cordle BOB Davidson BOB Zeni BRETT Myers BRIAN Burkett BRIAN MacDonald BRIANA Elsik
BRIGID Eduarte BRITTANY Campbell BRITTANY Klaus BRITTANY Martin Graunke BRUCE Leban BRYAN Shanaver
BRYAN Fenster CALEB Smagacz CALEB Brown CARL Catedral CARRIE Ballein CARSON Nyquist CHAD Hobson
CHARLES Lee CHARLIE Ridenour CHEN-Yao CHENG CHERI Hudspith CHIP & SHANNON Sohl CHRIS Miller CHRIS Paluch
CHRISTIANE Canfield CHRISTINA Moritz CHRISTOPHER Cole CHRISTOPHER Soloma de Cadavid CIARA Panacchia
COLLEEN Pratt CONNOR Regan DAN Cumberland DAN Portnoy DAN Powell DANIEL Boone DANIEL Cotter DANIEL Goldstein
DANIEL Kelleghan DANIELLE Gletow DANNY Feliciano DANNY Pettry DARIEN Gee DARREN Marshall DAVE &
HEATHER Berdan DAVE Hoover DAVID Gonzalez DAVID Chookaszian DAVID Katzman DAVID Melia DAWN Hancock
DEBI Augusty DEBORAH Alden DENISE Leok DEREK Wakefield DIANE Bergeson EDWARD Hirsch ELAINE Green
ELENA Bondar ELISA Doucette ELIZABETH Sorensen ELLEN Leanse ELLEN Miller ELLIOTT Day ELYSE Petersen EMILY Detroy
EMILY Goodrich EMILY Lautenbach ERIC Larkin ERIC Liechty ERICA Manami Juchems ERIN Hipp ERIN Kappelhof
EVA Penar FRANKLIN Sarkett MICHAEL Maddock GARIN Bulger GARRETT Witek GERRY True GISELE Nelson
GRANT Legan GREG Darley GREG Sabatos GREGORY Krieg GRETCHEN Dawley HENDRIKA Makilya HUGH Weber IAIN Boyd
ISSIS Saad JACK Berdan JACOB Ziech JAKE Nickell JAMES Shott JAN Oncken JANE Fitzgerald JARRETT Dawson
JASON Early JASON R. Yelm JEFF Cruz JEFF Goto JEFF Shinabarger JEN Marquez JEN Bachelder JEN Thomas
JEREMY Nelson JEREMY Painter JEREMY Worley JESSICA Rose Gann JESSICA Semaan JILL Felska JILLION Gislason
JINCE Kuruvilla JODI Casselberry JOE & AMANDA Cassidy JOE Cracchiolo JOE Faraoni JOE Varga JOHN Bergquist
JOHN Weeber JOHNATHON Strube JOHNNY Michael JON Crozier JON Svensson JOSH Hersh JOSH Cowman JOSH Burns
JOSH King JOSH Stewart JP Chookaszian JULIE Goding JUSTIN Ahrens KARLA Amador KATHY Kaminski KATIE Herman
KATIE Michels KELLY Kaminski KELLY Knaga KELLY O'Brien KELLY Pratt KELSEY Kreiling KENDEL Kirk KENDRA Olvany
KENNIS Negron KETURAH Kennedy KEVIN Von Qualen KIM Jones KIM Lichtenstein KIRK Chen KRISTEN Michelle Miller
KRISTIN Villa KYLE Ellman LACEY Edwards LARRY Stratton LAURA Gabriele LAUREN Mallen LEE Strawhun
LEI Liu LESLIE Slade LEVI M. Bulgar LINDA Hadfield LINDSAY Horwood LINSEY Burritt LIZ Carver LIZ Rose Chmela
LIZA Heavener LORI Webb LUCIA Dinh Pador LUCKA Zagorova LYNN Dickison MADISON Pucher MALLORI Kaminski
MARCELLA Brown MARCELO Sousa MARCO Garcia MARCOS Alcozer MARIAH Savage MARIO Mattei MARK Davenport
MARK Drozd MARK Hasell MARK Moll MARTA Garrido MARY Growney MATT Girgis MATT Johnson MATTHEW Hoffman
MATTHEW Straub MEGAN Richards Martin MEGHAN Lazier MEL Scott-Ticknor MELISSA Berger MELISSA Joy Kong
MELISSA Martens MELISSA Mashni MELISSA Saad MICHAEL Worley MIKE Ableman MIKE J. Zserdin MIKE McGee
MIKE Vallano MONA Nashed MUFFADAL Saylawala NATHAN Mead NATHAN Michael NAUSHEEN Qureshi NIC Lauten
NICK LeFors III NIKOLA Ranguelov NILES Emerick NILS NOAH Rothschild NYSA Vann PATRICIA McHugh PATRIK Byhmer
PATTY Huber PAUL Castronova PEGGY Casselberry PETER McBride PHIL Bridges PHIL EuBank POOJA Merai
PRESCOTT Van Leer PRINTNINJA RACHEL Doorags Vorm RAIKA Sarkett RANDY Chen RICK Zwetsch RILEY Oncken
RILEY Yoshiaki Masunaga ROB Gard ROB Modzelewski ROBBIE Abed ROBERT Hipp ROBIN Cornett ROCCO Capra
ROMAN Randall ROZILYN Bryant RYAN Potter RYAN Edwards RYAN Fitzgibbon RYAN Lazarus RYAN Mead RYAN Medina
RYAN Moore RYAN Sisson RYAN Vet SAM Rosen SAMUEL Ryan SAMUEL Stubblefield SARA Strawhun SARAH Alexander
SARAH Cole Kammerer SARAH Hatter SARAH Hurlburt SARAH Knotts SAYA Hillman SCOTT Hackman SCOTT Motte
SETH Kravitz SHANNON Downey SHARBEL Shamoon SHAWN Glanville STEPHEN Klueber STEVE Batterson STEVE Wellington
STEVEN Gallaher SUSAN Fezzey SUSAN Graunke TAMIE Jackson TAO Neuendorffer Flaherty TARA L. Rumler TIM Ghali
The FOLD The STUTTERING PROJECT THIRDINLINE CREATIVE THOMAS Hoffmann THOMAS I Koeplin THOMAS Tonder
TIJMEN Rumke TIM Naylor TIM Schraeder TIM Watson TODD TODD Pinckney TOM McNally TOM Schmitendorf
TONY Granados TORI Reneker TRAVIS Scott Collier TYLER Jackson TYLER Savage VAL Chulamorkodt VERONICA Garcia
VIKRAM WADE Roush ZACH Smith ZHENIA Koval

EXPERIENCE INSTITUTE

Higher education is changing.

My desire to learn how to practically and creatively make a difference in the world led me to launch The Leap Year Project. For the next year, my classrooms included creative spaces and offices, and my professors ranged from entrepreneurs to friends. Throughout the project, I realized that we had stumbled on a refreshing way to learn.

Experience Institute is the product of that realization.

The goal is to offer a place where people can learn through experiences as we begin building bridges between universities, employers, and future leaders.

By combining apprenticeships, conferences, volunteer experiences, and workshops, Experience Institute will provide an education that equips individuals with the tools necessary to transform our world with an inventive spirit.

For more information, *visit us at*
WWW.EXPINSTITUTE.COM

SAY HELLO

@VictorSaad
www.victorsaad.com

JOIN THE LEAP YEAR COMMUNITY

@LYProject
www.leapyearproject.org

GO TO SCHOOL

@ExpInstitute
www.expinstitute.com

ACKNOWLEDGEMENTS

There are so many people I wish to thank for inspiring and helping to create this book.

Thanks to Kelly Kaminski for directing the project with me. Grip Design for bringing our stories to life one page at a time. Tyler Savage, Michelle Lincoln, Ben Skoda, and Johnny Michael for months of early mornings and late nights. My Tang for managing the details. Sam Rosen and The COOP for providing space for us to work. Iain Boyd for your wise words and allowing me to use The Glass House. Alex Bogusky for writing the foreword and advising me along the way. Debbie Millman, Justin Ahrens, Brady Bone and Hendrika Makilya for the poster designs. The array of photographers who captured Leapers' stories around the world: Daniel Kelleghan, Grant Legan, Kevin Von Qualen, Michael Spataro, Caryn Werner, Alex Catedral, Stephanie Kunes, Sean Young, Hailey Hardin, Aaron Green, Jim Hardison, Sarah Cole Kammerer, Stephanie Bassos, Wei Shi, Vincent Cabansag, Michelle Marie, Ray Rushing, and Brian MacDonald.

And to the dozens of people who allowed me to work in your spaces, live in your homes, and share this journey...

Thank you.

TOGETHER, WE'VE INSPIRED REMARKABLE LEAPS AND CONNECTED AMAZING PEOPLE. WE'VE SPARKED POSITIVE ACTION IN CATEGORIES THAT RANGE FROM FARMING TO FAMILY AND WE'VE DONE IT THROUGH GOOD FRIENDSHIPS AND HARD WORK.

I HOPE, MORE THAN ANYTHING, THAT ALL OF THIS WAS JUST THE BEGINNING.

HERE'S TO YOU, LEAPERS.